I0134011

British Battlefields by Philip Warner
Volume 5 – Wales

Where the battles were fought
Why they were fought
How they were won and lost

Index of Contents

Notes on Map References

All Ordnance Survey maps are overlaid with an arrangement of numbered lines called the grid system, which enables any point of a map to be easily and accurately identified.

A map reference is given in two sets of three figures, for example 396 112. The first two figures of each trio (39 and 11) are the vertical line (northings) and the horizontal line (eastings) respectively; they intersect in the south-west (bottom left) comer of the square to which they refer. Smaller divisions of the square are not marked but may be estimated, and the third figures of each trio (6 and 2) represent the 'tenths' of the lines east and north (right and upwards). Thus 396 112 indicates a point six-tenths east and two-tenths north of the intersection of northing 39 and easting 11. Appendix 7 details, chapter by chapter, the ordnance survey maps which cover the areas in which the battles, skirmishes and campaigns described in this book took place.

In order to make the text understandable and acceptable to the widest circle of readers a compromise spelling has been adopted. Where possible a name is given in its Welsh spelling, e.g. Owain Glyndwr, Llywelyn. However, so that there may be no confusion, anglicized spelling is occasionally used, e.g. Griffith and Owen (as in Owen Gwynedd). Many readers would be baffled by the Welsh form of place names like Swansea (Abertawe) or Carmarthen (Caerfyrddin), so the English form is given.

'Ap' means 'son of'. Sometimes this is blended into the following name thereby creating a new form, e.g. Ap Rice = Price; Ap Richard = Pritchard.

In recent years the Welsh have altered the spelling 'Caernavon' to 'Caernafon' and 'Conway' to 'Conwy' (traditional Welsh forms), thus replacing the anglicized forms which appear in earlier writings (which also have the spelling 'Carnavon'). However these changes make no difference to the identification of the places mentioned in the text, so we have retained the forms which will be more familiar to tourists. Certain areas have also restored the former county names, e.g. Denbighshire, Flintshire, Pembrokeshire and Monmouthshire, and more are under consideration.

HOWEVER these name changes will not affect the visitor who will easily reach the battle sites in this book by means of the map references and road numbers provided. Wales contains numerous tourist offices and The Wales Tourist Board, Dept WMi, Davis Street, Cardiff CFi 2FU provides an excellent, free magazine guide which includes a comprehensive list of hotels and guest houses.

INTRODUCTION – British Battlefields

Very few living men have taken part in a battle, and many must wonder how they would acquit themselves if ever they had to.

A medieval battle was a very complex affair; it was far from being a simple matter of kill or be killed. It could be won or lost at any stage; it could turn on the action of one man, and not necessarily a man of high rank either, and it could settle nothing, or alternatively the fate of a nation.
But for the majority, when thinking of a battle, the overriding question would be: how would I behave? What would happen to me? Would I emerge unscathed and join in the celebrations, or would I be left wounded on the battlefield waiting for someone to save me, or for some ghoul to finish me off? Would I lose all fear in the excitement?

In reading the descriptions in this book it may be possible to guess the answers to some of those questions. On some of these battlefields you may feel luckier than on others. When you visit them it is worth bearing in mind that your own relations fought on these fields. This is almost certain. Everyone has two parents, four grandparents, sixteen great-grandparents ...and so on. If you work this out you may be sure that in any battle described in these books you probably had a number of ancestors fighting on each side. Doubtless they held a wide variety of ranks.

What were your chances? Battles are very strange. A wise commander does not give battle till he is sure he can win; some do not do so until they feel they have won already. Even today your estimate of why a former battle was won may be as good as anyone else's, for it is a strange fact about battles that often men do not know why they were won. The fact that one side had more casualties than the other means little. Most of the slaughter took place when one side had decided all was lost. The number killed when the battle was being fought may be small.

In examining these battlefields, and assessing the general situation, you must put yourself in the position of one of the senior commanders. You must remember how many troops you have and consider their quality. Are they well-trained, and well-armed? If not, are they well led? Do the junior commanders know their job? Will they keep their heads, take their men to the right objectives, control them in apparent victory, rally them in apparent defeat? Are they all going to be in their right places at the right time? What are their weapons like? Are the men skilled in their use? Many hundred years ago, in the declining years of the Roman Empire, a strategist wrote: 'A handful of men inured to war proceed to certain victory, while on the contrary numerous armies of raw and undisciplined troops are but multitudes of men dragged to slaughter.' It is as true today as it was then.

There were fashions in warfare, just as there were fashions in everything else, and sometimes a military fashion could be as impracticable as any other. On occasion armies were defeated because their commanders were relentlessly obstinate about moving with the times. In the first battle of this book we shall see how cavalry and bowmen won a battle against infantrymen but this led to an over-emphasis on the value of cavalry and neglect of infantry.

The axe was despised by the Normans because the Saxons used it, but became a very fashionable weapon for Normans later. The doom of the armoured knight eventually came from the longbow which was in use at the time of Hastings but in remote parts of Wales only. Whatever plans commanders make for battle they are -as often as not – thrown into disarray by unpredictable happenings on both sides. Confusion soon settles down on a battlefield and it is the commander who in that fast-changing, dangerous situation can think constructively and clearly who wins. The atmosphere of muddle which settles on to a battlefield is known as 'the fog of war'. The terms 'strategy' and 'tactics' are used loosely nowadays, and applied to so many non-military matters, that their proper meaning tends to be blurred. Strategy means the overall plan of a campaign for the defeat of an army, nation and people. Strategy requires you to mobilize all your resources, not only of people but also of food and weapons and equipment. It involves organizing the use of land, sea, and air transport, the use of propaganda, the preparation of de- tailed plans for a campaign and the provision of contingency plans against the unexpected. Just as it tries to organize its own resources it will try to disorganize the opposition. Nowadays, propaganda designed to upset enemy morale can be disseminated through radio, press and television. In the past it was done by spreading rumours through infiltrators. Rumours – particularly of bad news – spread very rapidly. The most morale-destroying rumour is that the commander-in-chief has prematurely departed from the field. In at least two of the battles described here commanders killed their horses at the outset with a view to showing that they themselves would stay to the end, whatever the probable result.

Strategy might or might not be influenced by the nature of the ground; tactics undoubtedly would be. Tactics is the science of the layout of troops in the face of the enemy and their use in action. Minor tactics deals with the problems occurring to sub-units, which maybe of patrol strength. However, it must not be thought that minor tactics are of little account. Skill in minor tactics is vital to success in a campaign. Strategy and tactics were not invariably the reason why battles were fought, for some occurred by accident; but strategy, if not tactics, brought the opposing armies to the point at which battle was joined. Both were in turn influenced by the physical features of the countryside. Very often these might be overlooked. It is obvious that armies have to take into account; mountains, hills, rivers, roads, swamps, forest, or very rough ground. What is less obvious is the influence of much smaller physical features. The battle of Poitiers in France 1356 was won by the Black Prince because the English could not be dislodged from a twenty-foot high hill protected by a hedge and a ditch; at the battle of Agincourt in 1415 the French lost because they tried to advance over newly-ploughed fields which were sodden from the recent rains. But battles may be lost for even less obvious reasons. A tree might serve as a rallying point, as an observation post, or as the cause of the split in the advance of an army; a stream might enable an army and its horses to refresh themselves, or might lead to its defeat. When on a battlefield it is advisable to look for every tiny rivulet and patch of marshy ground. As that rivulet was trampled in and clogged with bodies it could soon become a marsh, and then a miniature lake. Woe betide anyone who was pushed back into it, particularly if he was wearing heavy armour. On some battlefields you will find a site marked 'Bloody Meadow'. A glance at the surrounding topography will show how it obtained its chilling name.

A stream might have been dammed before the battle began in order to make the enemy advance on a very narrow front. This would nullify an advantage in numbers. During the Zulu wars in the nineteenth century a handful of Dutch held back thousands of Zulus because the latter could not reach them; the place was subsequently known as 'Blood River'. Kenilworth Castle, which does not look particularly formidable today, was once made impregnable by the damning of two small streams; it was then surrounded by 111 acres of water.

Control of an area is made effective by a commander being able to move forces rapidly from one part to another. Thus you will find battlefields near roads or rivers, or *nodal points* as junctions of either are called. For the same reason you will find the entrance to valleys, or passes, or bridges and fords, all bear traces of nearby fortifications. It is all too easy to underrate these fortifications because many people merely see them as inert defences which would be dangerous within arrow range only. On the contrary they were bases, and although built to give a good account of themselves if besieged, would mainly be used to house fighters who would tackle the opposition just as they emerged out of the river or perhaps before they were in sight of the fortification. The problem of a fortification, however small, to an advancing army, was that it would be too great a threat yet might take time to reduce. And time might be a vital commodity. Delay might prevent an army reaching a vital river crossing before it was strongly defended, might prevent it from capturing a town which held vital stores, or might prevent a link-up with other forces, converging from different directions.

The sites of battles are then anything but haphazard. But before being able to predict why and where battles must have been fought you need to investigate what changes have taken place in the countryside between the date of the battle and today. It may surprise you. What is now dry ploughland may once have been wet tussocky scrubland, the battlefield may perhaps have a town built on it but even then there are probably tell-tale signs. But even if the surface of the battlefield has been largely obliterated the surrounding area will do much to explain it. You will soon learn to recognise the importance of certain features – or 'develop an eye for ground'. With a little practice you will be able to estimate where the attack came from before even looking at the detailed map. You will make mistakes. You will perhaps forget the time it takes to move men over encumbered ground; it is no good saying 'he should have attacked on the flank' if the approach would have been thick with bodies and abandoned equipment. You will probably try to squeeze too many men into too small an area- as many a commander has done before you. You will perhaps neglect your cavalry, or your artillery. In assessing what you yourself might have done you must accept completely what the enemy did do. Your version of the battle may prove more successful than your predecessor's – or less.

Battles, in the times we speak of, lasted but a day. Pursuit and slaughter may have taken longer but the decision would be reached in a matter of hours. Siege battles were, of course, a different story. The explanation of the shortness of early battles lies in the weapons they used. Draw a bow a hundred times and see how much longer you want to go on for. Take a sword, or a billhook, and try hacking a way through a copse for an hour.

Better still, pad yourself up with protective clothing before you begin and move rapidly from place to place. Even then you will lack the noise, the effect of cavalry changes sending a shock through the ranks, and the bruises that often came from the weapons of friends as well as foes. But you will be getting the feel of a medieval battle.

Introduction to Volume 5, Wales

The battlefields of Wales are unlike those of most other countries. There are no Nasebys or Floddens or Cullodens in Wales, which may seem surprising as the Welsh have always been a martial people. There are battlefields, of course, but they are small ones and often they are killing grounds chosen by the guerrilla fighter. The Welsh have always had a clear grasp of strategy and tactics and had much too much sense to be caught on battlefields where they would be at a disadvantage. Their best allies were mountains and rivers which they used to good advantage. In fact, if you ask a Welshman whether he recalls any famous Welsh battles, as likely as not he will be unaware of his country's military history and instead will give a detailed description of his favourite Rugby team in some Homeric encounter: Newport against Cardiff perhaps, or Llanelli battling it out with Swansea. Better still, it may be a lesser known team contending with one of the great ones. And if he describes such an occasion – before you can stop him getting into his stride – he will, unknown to him but not to you, be reciting all the strength and weakness of the Welsh. He will mention the initial tactical plan without which no Welsh team ever sets foot on the field, even though it may never be followed. He will mention the heroes in awed tones and, as the story unfolds, you will note that the small were never afraid to challenge the large, that resource, flexibility and speed were the order of the day, that narrow defeat could quickly be turned into rout and that the result was in the balance till the final moment. In Rugby football or in war the Welsh have an extraordinary facility for producing something new or unexpected at some stage in the encounter. Only a foolish opponent will see himself gaining an advantage and confidently await an easy victory. There are no easy victories over the Welsh, at war or at play, as many a redoubtable gladiator has found.

Welsh soldiers are familiar enough with large set-piece battlefields and they have acquitted themselves with distinction on them. Mention of this will be made later. The Welsh have fought in a variety of armies, sometimes as allies and sometimes as mercenaries. Today the word 'mercenary' has a denigratory connotation. It was not always so. In earlier centuries the soldier of fortune who gave his skill, and often his life, did so not merely for pay but for his leader. It was a contract. The leader who hired him gave him his pay and was expected to preserve his life if possible; the soldier in his turn would honour his obligation to give of his best up to death if need be. In the French Revolution Louis XVI's Swiss Guard died for him, although it would have been easy to avoid doing so. In 1102, when Bridgnorth Castle was under siege, the mercenaries of the rebel baron Belesme refused to give in and gave Henry I exceptional trouble. There are many examples of mercenaries proving more loyal and reliable to their hirer than local native troops proved to be. Perhaps the best tribute to mercenaries was that paid by the Romans who rewarded them, at the end of their service, with Roman citizenship.

Welsh mercenaries were greatly esteemed and widely feared in the Middle Ages. The word 'Welsh' was almost synonymous with 'longbow' and the longbow was the great battle-winning weapon for two centuries. Of that more later.

But with all this goes the fact that the Welsh are somewhat of a mystery, even to themselves. Even today, when thousands of tourists visit Wales every year, when thousands of Welshmen work and live in England, when Welsh problems are fully and freely discussed in the press, and on radio and television, there is still something inscrutable about the people of Wales.

Militarily the Welsh have often proved to be their own worst enemies. All too often, gains made by desperate fighting and unlimited courage were frittered away, or even bartered, because of petty rivalries and jealousies. It is, of course, easier to hate your immediate neighbour, the occupant of the next valley, whose family has been stealing from yours (when you were not stealing from his) for many a year. It was as well for the enemies of Wales that this was so, but suicidal for the Welsh themselves.

The story of warfare in Wales spans some three thousand years. Most of the earlier battles are known only by traces on the ground and even many of the later ones were imperfectly recorded. It is, of course, unrealistic to expect an impartial and factual account of an early battle. Numbers engaged and casualties suffered are either exaggerated or diminished and even the site of the battle may be a matter for dispute. However, it is surprising how much may be deduced from scanty and vague records if one visits the probable sites and assesses the available accounts. For, the fact is, you cannot fight a battle anywhere. A good general only fights a battle when he considers it to be already won. His opponents may have no choice but usually one side will have judged the terrain suitable for its tactical plan. It may be somewhere very small, such as a river crossing suitable for an ambush, or it may be at the neck of a valley where an unwary opponent can easily become trapped; it may, on occasion, be a wide flat plain where the man who has chosen it plans to make full use of his cavalry. There are, indeed, a few battlefields where armies stumble on each other by chance and fight it out then and there while each is trying to obtain the maximum advantage from this unexpected, and usually unwanted, encounter. This was always liable to happen in earlier centuries when neither side had proper maps, compasses, or timepieces. But such unwanted occasions were surprisingly few. In most battles one, and sometimes both, of the commanders would have approved the site as fitting in with his resources and tactical plan.

× battles or skirmishes

■ sieges

First a look at the military geography of Wales. A line of mountains runs north to south, approximately 150 miles long. Snowdon, the highest of the peaks, is to the northwest and the range of which it is a part runs roughly northeast to south-west. South-east of Snowdon we come to Plynlimmon. All the western side of Wales is mountainous but in the central areas there are gaps of fertile land. This combination of mountains, hills and remote valleys made Wales an excellent place of refuge but at the same time it was exceptionally difficult for those living in the area to develop any form of unity.

In prehistoric times when people lived in comparatively small tribal groups, lack of unity was not important. There was probably very little fighting at all, unlike the Iron Age. The men of the palaeolithic, or Old Stone Age, a period approximately from 500,000 to 9000 BC, may never have turned their weapons against each other: their arrowheads and axes, which we still discover, were for obtaining food by killing wild animals. They were cave dwellers, and apparently built no fortifications. Apart from tools they left traces of their presence in the form of pictures drawn on the walls of their caves; however, there are few traces of palaeolithic man in Wales, although he must have lived there.

In the Middle Stone Age (Mesolithic period) which extends from 9000 to 4000 BC, there were a number of people on the mountains of Wales who left relics of their presence in the shape of the barbs and arrow heads used for killing wild animals and fishing. Again, it is unlikely that they turned their weapons against each other. All these early peoples appear to have been nomadic. In the Old Stone Age they may be traced from the north of Europe and Scandinavia; in the Middle Stone Age they came from Africa. In what is known as the New Stone Age (Neolithic period), roughly from 4000 to 1500 BC, there was an incursion by another group of people who originated from as far afield as the eastern Mediterranean but who had lived for a time in northern Europe, as they made their slow progress to Wales. Movement was slow, people might travel only a few miles in a hundred years, but what is a hundred years in ten thousand? These later arrivals did not change ground as often as their predecessors had done, for basic cultivation of wheat and barley was now practised. Animals were kept in herds and grazed wherever grass could be made to grow. The cattle were protected from wild animals by what are called causewayed camps. These camps were usually on or near hilltops and consisted of an enclosure protected by one or more ditches. Although initially for use against wild animals, many were later adapted for use against hostile humans. It may seem surprising that primitive people should have taken so much trouble to dig out these huge ditches when a Zareba type of enclosure seemingly would have served as well. However, our remote ancestors may have learnt from experience that wild animals, such as wolves or bears, have a wonderful facility for climbing any form of fence. Consequently intruders could only be kept out by vertical walls with, probably, water-filled ditches outside them.

Primitive fortifications look misleadingly simple today, with their gentle grass-covered slopes; however, when they were built the slopes were made vertical and the ditches were much deeper than nowadays. With fortifications, whether against humans or animals, it is useless to adopt half measures, and that was a mistake our ancestors never made. When their fortifications failed to keep out an invader it was not through lack of will but only through lack of means. From this period too, date the great tombs known as cromlechs, which were usually made of two or three upright stones roofed with a huge capstone. How these great capstones were manoeuvred into position is not known, but it was probably in much the same way as the massive stones of Stonehenge were eased into place. Excavation inside henges shows that they were centres for cremation and burial. Neolithic men built long barrows or gallery graves. There are many of these in north-west Wales and Anglesey. They also built passage graves – round earth mounds with a passage into the interior, of which there is an excellent example at Bryn Celli Ddu on Anglesey. The passage is 26 feet long, and the mound 12 feet high and 90 feet in diameter. Barclodiad, also on Anglesey, is slightly smaller. Although not in Wales, the Silbury Hill mound, near Marlborough, Wiltshire, will intrigue those interested in these monuments. Its size is astonishing and the visitor will not be surprised to hear that it is the largest artificial mound in Europe. It is 130 feet high and 120 feet in diameter. Although it has been excavated, there is nothing to explain its size or purpose. There is, however, no doubt that it was built at approximately 2000 BC.

The next arrivals were the Beaker folk. Their name is derived from the drinking vessels they used, which were of an unusual type with the sides slightly convex-like a bell. Their main claim to fame is the building of Stonehenge, but they had other accomplishments than building henges and it is known that they wore woollen clothes, used copper, and even practised brain surgery. There had been a Henge at Stonehenge before the Beaker folk arrived but they extended it by a double circle of bluestones. The remarkable feature of these bluestones is that they had been quarried as far away as the Preseli (Prescelly) mountains in Dyfed. The Preseli mountains were perhaps regarded as sacred mountains and this may have justified the prodigious labour of cutting the stones, dragging them on rollers to the coast, transporting them up the Bristol Avon to Frome, partly dragging them and partly transporting them slung under rafts on the Wylye and finally manoeuvring them into exact position on the site. Visitors to Stonehenge marvel at the thought of a primitive people being able to build such a monument. Those who know how far the stones journeyed and what mathematical calculation would have been required throughout the operation, will scarcely regard these remote ancestors of ours as primitive. There are other henges of this date and they include Trecastle and Cerig-Duon in Powys and Gors Fawr in Dyfed. It is thought that some of the more elaborate architectural ideas, such as mortice and tenon joints, show a link with the Greeks but the contact may be with only one, or perhaps a few, of the Greek architects of that period.

As the late neolithic and Beaker folk period merges into the Bronze Age, 1600 BC to about 700 BC, we reach the time when man is not merely in conflict with nature and animals but with his fellow men. Bronze is a mixture of copper and tin and, as an alloy, is tougher than either, but the people of the Bronze Age also used gold and amber. Perhaps it was possession of the two latter which brought men into conflict, for we now find an assembly of weapons: battleaxes, knives and arrowheads, buried in tombs. In the bell-shaped barrows in which Bronze Age man was buried we find different grades of person. Chiefs or local kings had rich furnishings interred with them and around were the lesser graves of their warriors.

After iron smelting had been discovered, in approximately 700 BC, its use spread rapidly. With it there emerged a pattern in society which was to endure for over two thousand years. It was a form of feudalism in which those who had grown rich by farming, fighting or trading were able to employ others and be their chieftains. The enclosures which had formerly been used to protect herds against wild animals were now used to protect the chieftain and his dependants against those with whom he had quarrelled. In peaceful times the tenants would farm the land on the slopes of the hill but when danger threatened all would take refuge in what now became a hill fort.

Although the main age of the hill fort is 500–100 BC, it would be optimistic to imagine that occasional clashes had not occurred much earlier. Even in the Stone Age when there seemed to be enough room for everyone there must have been occasions when the arrival of newcomers provoked hostility. However, for the most part, life seems to have been peaceful. But to judge from the large numbers of forts constructed in the Iron Age a very different, and unneighbourly, attitude seems to have been the rule. Hill forts, sometimes known as contour forts because they frequently followed the contours of the hill, consisted not merely of the deep ditches and tall earthworks which remain today but also stockades, elaborate gateways, defensive outworks and cunningly constructed traps. A hill fort could use ten thousand tree trunks in one line of ramparts alone and some had two or three. There are over two thousand hill forts in England and Wales and they vary from the vast area of Maiden Castle, Dorset, to quite small enclosures. As the years passed the stronger chieftains grew stronger and extended their territories, creating behind a system of dykes what we would now call an estate. In the graves of these chieftains and their warriors we find a variety of the implements of war: axes, long swords, and shields.

In Wales we find relics of all the peoples mentioned above, the Stone Age peoples, the Bronze Age and the Iron Age. These invaders who had come from distant parts of Europe and the Middle East wandered across England and, often making way for the next wave of invaders, settled in Wales or in Ireland. Small wonder that the Welsh are such a complex people. They are an amalgam of so many different stocks that it is to be expected that conflict of ideas and loyalties may exist even in a Welshman's own mind. Nor can it be wondered at that the inhabitants of one area might find some difficulty in co-operating with the denizens of another; their origins and philosophy might be quite different. There were, of course, a number of shared characteristics. All the invaders of the Stone Age and early Bronze Age period are roughly classed as Iberians, for they were short, dark, and long-skulled, apt at intricate arts and dexterous. This dark stocky type is to most foreigners the natural Welshman, but this is an illusion: there are other equally natural Welsh types. Nevertheless the Iberian flint miner, who chipped out flint arrowheads – often as sharp as a modem steel knife – was the precursor of the Welsh bowman of the Middle Ages and the Welsh miner and craftsman of the industrial era. The other type of Welshman is no less 'natural'. He was tall, fair-haired and blue-eyed. He began to settle in Wales as early as 1000 BC. He was the Celt. He brought bronze and iron with him but that was not the only reason why he be-came a conqueror. Whereas the Iberian was placid and un- aggressive, the Celt set out to dominate and subdue. He was bold, dashing and impatient. He was much admired- not least by himself. The Iberian accepted the Celt at his own valuation but later when Saxons, Romans and English tried to force their way into Wales, it was the Iberian stock which produced the toughest and most enduring resistance. But it should not be assumed that these people were homogeneous. Both Iberians and Celts had conflicts between themselves. Ultimately, Wales seems to have fallen into four main areas of tribal influence. Gwynedd, which includes Snowdon, was the Deceangli realm; Powys, which includes the Berwyn range, was the territory of the Ordovices; the Demetae dominated modem Dyfed, and the southern area was the land of the Silures. Much to the surprise of people living outside Wales, the names of Dyfed, Powys, Gwynedd, and others such as Gwent, now appear on modem maps. They have replaced the names of smaller administrative areas such as Denbigh, Brecon, Pembrokeshire, etc. A tourist who finds this confusing may take comfort from the fact that the names at least have a historic value, unlike the bureaucratic imposition in England of such names as Humberside, Cleve-land, and West Midlands – names as barren and cumbersome as the minds of those who imposed them on the public.

That the Celtic invasion started Wales on a path of warfare is obvious from the number and variety of die hill forts. On the coasts there were promontory forts, but inland there were forts made on crags, forts with stone walls, and forts with deep ditches; sometimes all defensive methods were combined on the same site. Many are small, enclosing a mere 2–3 acres. Around them you may trace field patterns by the fact that over the years stones were carefully carried to the sides, thus clearing the centre and also forming a boundary line. As you stand on the perimeter of one of these hill forts you will be aware that this place was once a minor battlefield. Such forts were not built for ornament, nor were they untested. Standing in an Iron Age fort, it is not difficult to tell from which direction the main threat came nor how it was countered. And if you hear – or should be speaking – Welsh or Cornish or Breton, the language is the language that the warriors of that day used as they urged each other to the final effort which brings victory if you are fortunate, or defeat if you are unlucky.

Two further points are of interest to those wishing to understand the make-up of the Welsh nation and thus of its military ideology. One was the incursion, in the third century bc, of what is called the La Tene culture. Typical of these people was a form of decoration used on metal-work, which was usually very ornate. It appears on helmets, shields, scab-bards, swords, and axes, as well as on many less military objects. When a weapon becomes a work of art it acquires a special value and significance. The elaborate and extremely expensive decoration on some shotguns today is an example. These Iron Age invaders are sometimes known as the Mamians, as they previously lived in the Marne area. However, they were not unlike the Hallstatt people. One of their tribes which settled in Yorkshire was known as the Parisii. They were, as were most Celts, experts in chariot warfare; women had equal status with men, became chieftains and led their armies to battle. The second factor is the Belgae invasion in the first century bc. The Belgae were a mixture of Celt and Teuton. They had resisted the Romans in Gaul and would resist them even more strenuously on this side of the Channel. One of their tribes was the Catuvellauni, which means 'the mighty warriors'. Among the skills of the Celtic tribes was phenomenal ability with the sling. The sling is a useful weapon for it can take a variety of ammunition, can maintain a continuous rapid flow of missiles over a long period, and is easily carried. It is not affected by weather as a bowstring will be and its ammunition, unlike arrows or bullets, is easily available. At Maiden Casde there was a dump of twenty thousand slingstones. Furthermore, a slingstone is in many ways like a howitzer shell; its trajectory carries it over ramparts and trenches and kills those walking inside. The slingstone made defence in depth a necessity.

In the later period of the Iron Age (c.100 bc) the Druid religion seems to have been powerful and widespread. Celtic religion venerated a number of natural objects, such as certain trees, springs, rivers, rocks, or woods. Reincarnation was a part of Celtic belief. Priests, who served a long apprenticeship, were very powerful but sacrificed human beings frequently to the gods who were even more powerful. When the Romans invaded Britain the Druids were gradually forced back into Wales until their last stronghold was destroyed by Paulinus in Anglesey in AD 60. However, even after their destruction in open battles the Druids continued to operate as a driving force in local resistance.

Other tribes also found refuge in Wales during the period of Roman rule. Among them were the Brigantes, who had settled in the north of England. The Romans drove them out of England but the Brigantes moved to Tre'r Ceiri, a large hill fort in Gwynedd, where they remained throughout the Roman occupation of Britain; doubtless there were many battles around this site.

The meet important ancient forts in Wales are the following:

On Anglesey: Caer Leb, an earthwork which mostly dates from the third century AD but which is on an earlier defensive site, Caer Twr, an Iron Age hill fort on the top of Holyhead mountain, and Castell Bryn Gwyn, just west of Llaniban. Castell Bryn Gwyn is neolithic but was also used later.

In Powys: Castell Dinas, an Iron Age hill fort with a Norman motte inside it (near Crickhowell).

In Gwynedd: Iron Age hill forts at Dinas Dinlle (one mile from Llandwrog) with double ramparts, and other forts close by at Craig y Dinas and Caer Engan. Tre'r Ceiri, close to Llanaelhhaean, has already been mentioned. Caer Drewyn, near Corwen, was an Iron Age hill fort which was later put to use by the Welsh resisting the invasion of Henry II.

In Dyfed the visitor will find an Iron Age fort just northeast of Tregaron, and a very fine example at Cam Engyl lie (sometimes spelt Camingli), near Fishguard Bay. Foel Trigam, in this area, has sophisticated entrances and there are many others which may be located by using the Ordnance Survey map 'Southern Britain in the Iron Age'. The tourist who knows a few words of Welsh will find this a great help in understanding place names. Caer and gaer both mean a fort, but cam and gam mean hill. Allt is a cliff, afon a river and aber a river mouth. Thus Caernarvon means a fort on a river. Bryn is a hill and mawr means large, bwlch means a pass and cefn a ridge. Crug is a mound and dinas another word for a fort. Tomens or domens are not forts but burial mounds. Nant is a stream. Clwyd means a gate, coed a wood, and cwm a valley. Carreg is a stone and castell is a castle. However, when an excavation takes place a Hen Domen (old burial mound) may turn out not to be a burial mound at all but the remains of a motte and bailey castle and Pen y Castell may not be a castle but an Iron Age fort.

Dinas Bran in Clwyd is an Iron Age fort with the remnants of a medieval castle on top of it. We shall have more to say of Dinas Bran later. It takes its name from the fact that a crow was supposed to build there every year. Dinas Bran overlooks Llangollen and a visitor who contemplates a little exercise will certainly obtain it if he clambers to the summit. Having done so, he will wonder how it could ever have been captured.

Although the effects of two thousand years of weathering have smoothed the lines of most Iron Age forts, it is not difficult to visualize their military potential. Particular attention should be paid to the entrance, for a valuable technique of military architecture, then and later, was to lure the intruder into a blind alley where he could be isolated and have his retreat cut off. It is said that many Iron Age forts were not continuously occupied; however, the size of most of them suggests that they could maintain the local population for a long period. Water was probably supplied by a system of dew ponds in summer; a dew pond is easily constructed by digging a flat depression, lining it with straw or another non-conductor, covering this and then letting it fill up. However, dew ponds would probably be inadequate for any lengthy occupation.

A feature which may seem remarkable nowadays is the size of the community effort which went into prehistoric buildings. There was a pattern to life which we do not understand because it has been eroded in much the same way as the pre-historic ramparts have been eroded. Clearly, vast community effort must have been needed to create the cromlechs, domens, forts and henges of ancient times. It seems unlikely that such constructions were the result of slave labour, except on a very few occasions. Undoubtedly, life in the community was enriched by ceremony. We can only see the results of this in their burial customs, but it is unlikely that all these ancient people merely had a necrophilic culture. In all probability the ceremonial inhumation or cremation of the dead was but one aspect of their lives. When tanks rumble past hill forts it is worth considering that though military thought has advanced, spiritual development has almost completely withered. In the modem world attendance at religious festivals or services has declined, the Church endeavours to follow materialistic views rather than lead, confidence in our divine origins and destiny has almost totally disappeared. Perhaps this is a mark of advancing civilization; perhaps not. Pagan though they were, these ancient people seem to have had more religious motivation, more community spirit and more joy in life than most people living today with every aid to happiness except the right attitude of mind.

One aspect of religious ceremonial in ancient Britain seems to have been overlooked but it might readily occur to a Welshman. Stonehenge, Avebury, and other sites could well have resounded with song just like the Eisteddfodd, Cardiff Arms Park and many other places where Welsh congregate. Perhaps the most pleasing feature of prehistoric life was that everyone could and did sing. The motivation which takes thousands to attend pop concerts in considerable discomfort, or to accompany Welsh Rugby teams to Twickenham and inspire them with traditional song, has perhaps a longer history than we imagine.

Chapter 2

THE BATTLES AGAINST THE ROMANS

Although the Romans had made a military reconnaissance in Britain in 55 and 54 BC, these campaigns were not intended as a proper military conquest. Nearly a hundred years elapsed before a full-scale invasion took place. It came in AD 43 when Aulus Plautius landed at Richborough, Kent, with four legions each numbering five thousand men; there was the same number of support troops. This army overran south-eastern Britain without great difficulty but ran into rather more trouble when it pushed north and west. In AD 47 Aulus Plautius returned to Rome and was replaced in due course by Ostorius Scapula. Ostorius Scapula was a talented leader but he faced a task which required all his abilities. The Romans had good reason to respect the Catuvellauni, whose power extended over most of the Midlands. Their capital was Camulodunum, named after Camulos, the god of war; this was Colchester. The Catuvellauni had been led very successfully by Cunobelinus, better known as Cymbeline, and now that he was dead his place had been taken by no less a man, his son Caratacus, as the Romans called him. Caratacus is variously known as Caractacus, Caratacas and Caradoc. An explanation of the variation in names follows later in this book. As a Briton his proper name was Caradoc, which we shall henceforth use. This was the man Ostorius Scapula had to conquer.

Although the Romans had vast superiority in trained troops and equipment they found Caradoc a major problem; he fought battle after battle with them and each time disengaged leaving them without the fruits of victory. Caradoc was in the great tradition of guerrilla warriors; it is hard even now to know where his main base was. However we do know enough of Caradoc to make some valid assumptions. By AD 47 he was not merely the chief of the Catuvellauni but also the accepted leader of all the other British tribes too.

Furthermore he had the spiritual backing of the Druids from their retreat in Anglesey. And the longer the Romans stayed in Britain the more support would resistance leaders receive from those whose territories the Romans had already overrun. The Romans were not unaware of this possibility and in order to prevent trouble in rear areas had decided to disarm tribes which had submitted on honourable terms and been granted the right to bear arms. The latter included the Iceni, who later would produce the renowned Boadicea (or Boudicca as some prefer). The Iceni rebelled against die forced disarmament in AD 48 but were rigorously suppressed. After this salutory lesson to the rear areas, Ostorius could now turn his attention to Wales, he thought; the Iceni, of course, thought otherwise. The Roman army left traces of its progress towards Wales in various ways. It left temporary marching camps and also practice camps for teaching or retraining troops in the art of war. It also left milestones, auxiliary forts, signal stations and military towns. Last, but by no means least, it left roads.

The Romans did not really wish to be involved in north Wales. South Wales was a different story, for there were very dear advantages to being in that area, but the north was a tangle of dangerous mountains where a legion could easily be cut off and destroyed. Ostorius decided the best route to the conquest of Wales was via Mold, Denbigh and St Asaph. This would take him straight to the heart of the Deceangli country without risking his forces in obvious ambush positions. However, as every practitioner of guerrilla warfare knows, it is one thing to invade an enemy's territory and another to bring one's opponent to battle and destroy him. All the guerrilla needs to do is to harass the invader and wait. In time the invasion force will need to restore its armaments, food and, probably, morale. So it withdraws with every intention of fighting another day.

On this occasion Ostorius had to retire prematurely from Wales because messengers brought him bad news. The Brigantes, a formidable tribe in Yorkshire, were up in arms and were liable to sweep across his line of communication and leave him and his army isolated in Wales. Besides there were more important problems than even Caradoc and his remote strongholds. South Wales was still to be conquered and although the territory there was less forbidding than the north, the Silures were no less indomitable than the other tribes of Wales. They might perhaps prove the most difficult of all.

In AD 50 Ostorius was ready to try again-on all fronts. From the camp at Gloucester a Roman army set off across the Severn, probing with some caution. Meanwhile from the Bristol Channel a fleet of Roman boats sailed along the south Wales coastline, not so much looking for landing points as assessing and attempting to intimidate the Silurian defenders. Ostorius's activities in the South Wales area were not overlooked by Caradoc. If the Romans had much success in that area two effects would be felt by the rest of Wales. The first was that Welsh morale would be greatly weakened, leading undoubtedly to criticism of Caradoc, who had taken no steps to prevent it; the second was that, after the Romans had subdued south Wales, they could overrun the north at their convenience, possibly using locally recruited troops, as they had done in other countries. In the course of time, events proved somewhat different.

Caradoc now took the offensive. He moved his headquarters south from the Deceangli territory into the Ordovices regions. It was a wise precaution. While he remained up in the extreme north the Romans could move up the lines of the Wye and the Usk, thereby gaining control of the main valley routes into central Wales. However, Caradoc needed to do more than make shrewd strategic and tactical moves; he needed a victory. And the sort of victory he needed was not a mere guerrilla skirmish but a slaughter in which Roman armies would be so mauled they would be glad to make a realistic peace as with an equal. Caradoc was doubtless aware of the Roman attitude to being embroiled in difficult and dangerous fighting in Wales. He may have assumed, probably rightly, that the Romans were content with holding the lowland areas of Britain and would accept the idea of a vassal king of Wales. Caradoc, however, may have had aspirations to being king of more than Wales and wished his kingdom to extend eastwards well into what would later become the English Midlands.

Whatever the boundaries of Caradoc's ambitions, he would need a clear-cut victory over a Roman army if he were to achieve them. The key to the conquest of north-west Britain and Wales was control of the Dee estuary. When it was achieved by the Ramans they signalled the fact by building a powerful fortress at Chester (Deva). The Roman plan was to have a chain of strong forts along what may roughly be called the Midland gap and those forts would be at Gloucester, Worcester, Viroconium (Wroxeter) and Chester. This opened up a route for penetration of the western side of the Pennines and at the same time enabled forces to find their way across north Wales to Anglesey – the spiritual home of British resistance.

Strategically this was entirely reasonable. There were, however, snags. The Roman army had made very little progress against the peoples of south Wales, and if an attack was launched from that area, on say Gloucester, this would be a devastating blow for Roman prestige. The Romans were experienced enough at warfare to calculate their chances nicely. When matters went according to their plan they could switch troops from main bases to marching camps and from marching camps to frontier posts. Whenever the Romans moved they dug in. In doubtful territory the day's march would be ended by midday and the rest of the daylight hours be spent fortifying the site. Perhaps the next morning the Romans might abandon that particular camp for ever, but that was better than themselves staying there for ever, caught by a surprise attack on an incomplete fortification. The Romans had learned their lessons the hard way and learned them well.

Caradoc had apparently decided the best fort for his pro-posed attack was Wroxeter. This abandoned town has now been excavated and should not be missed by a tourist. At Wroxeter Ostorius had stationed two legions, the 2nd and the 14th. With true Roman thoroughness Wroxeter was linked to Gloucester by the road which runs south through Droitwich and Worcester, and with near areas by the road which runs to Penkridge, and thus all the way to London. There was another more forward lateral road in the course of construction which would eventually link Caerleon, Abergavenny, Kenchester, Leintwardine, Wroxeter and Whitchurch. An efficient road system is always of great service to occupying powers and a threat to the plans of guerrilla leaders. The steady advance of this road network convinced Caradoc that there was no time to lose; the Romans must be taught that the cost of conquering Wales was too high.

The exact site of the ensuing battlefield has been the subject of much conjecture. In our view there is no doubt that it is the one described here but it is worth visiting other proposed sites as their reputation is undoubtedly based upon local tradition of a battle once being fought there and also a topography which matches the basic account given by Tacitus. However, Tacitus left as such a minimal account that his outline would fit nearly a hundred possible sites. One of these is the Llanidloes area, probably at Cefncamedd. In recent years archaeologists have discovered marching camps at Brompton and it may be that the Romans were already penetrating Wales along the line of the Severn. However, this seems improbable and it is more than likely that the camps were established after the Caradoc battle when an attempt was being made to dominate the new territories. Yet another favoured site is Dolferwyn Castle. Tacitus's all too brief account refers to the spirit of the British 'which dismayed the Roman commander'. A river flowed in front of the position, 'of uncertain or doubtful depth'. Behind was a craggy eminence on top of which was a fortress. The 'fortress' may have been of wood.

The most significant clue to identifying this battlefield is the fact that there are two Caer Caradocs near to Wroxeter. Both incidentally happen to be in what is now Shropshire, but many centuries would elapse before a border area was clearly defined. As with all border areas or 'marches' to this day-whether between England and Wales or England and Scotland, or on many frontier areas in other countries, there is a notable blending of people; it is not always easy to recognise from name or accent which side of the line it is on. There is incidentally another Caer Caradoc much further north that must date from Caradoc's time with the Deceangli.

One Caer Caradoc is two miles north-east of Church Stretton (Sheet 137: 478 955); another, also on Sheet 137 is at 310 758. The latter, near Pentre, has claims to be considered as a battle site, although the river Redlake, even in flood, seems a little narrow to fit Tacitus's eloquent description. (It is, of course, a well-known phenomenon that battles described by the victors tend to exaggerate the depth and width of the rivers they crossed, the steepness of the hills they climbed, and the fierceness of the opposition.) Nevertheless, we feel it probable, as also did that eminent and astute military historian, the late Lt-Col A. H. Bume, that the battle site was more likely to be midway between the two points than actually on one of them. Caradoc, incidentally, did not construct any of the three forts which bear his name: they have been dated to an earlier period. However, undoubtedly he used them. They gave him an excellent opportunity to harass any Roman force with ambitions to penetrate Wales along the line of the Clun river. An ideal place to intercept the Romans would be at the foot of Clunbury Hill, probably at the point 375 805. The River Clun is joined by the River Kemp here and in AD 51 this would have been a very marshy and uncertain area. There is no better place for taking on a heavily armed adversary than on marshy ground which he does not know and you do.

The Romans could, of course, have marched right through the position and avoided conflict on such an exacting site. However that was not the Roman way and furthermore there was a strong possibility that Caradoc had slipped another force on to the road behind in case the Romans felt a strategic withdrawal would be wise. The Romans, undoubtedly, were caught in a trap. If they moved they would know that they must fight a battle sooner or later and the next challenge might come on an even worse site-if that were possible. If they retreated they lost a golden chance to bring the British to battle and defeat them. Caradoc had undoubtedly read their minds aright.

Thus we can picture the scene. The Romans, strong, experienced and well-trained (they did arms drill for eight hours a day), were determined to defeat Caradoc and glad to be meeting him in open battle. Caradoc, feeling he had drawn his opponents into a trap, would be equally determined that this would be the end of Roman power in the north-west.

In the year AD 51 the Clun was a larger river than it is today; this has been established by the size of the channel. Apart from the extra volume of water it carried it would be an awkward hazard, for until comparatively recent times rivers sprawled across the landscape, partly dammed by fallen trees and other obstacles.

The task of negotiating the treacherous shallows and depths of the river must have caused heavy losses to the Romans, for the Britons would find them easy targets for their sling shot. However, of the probable 15,000 Romans, a good proportion would soon have crossed the river and be forcing a way up the slope. It is believed that the Britons had constructed some form of stockade close to the river bank so that they could spear the advancing Romans without too great cost to themselves. Behind this, and higher up the hill, was another barrier. As both must have been of wood and thorn, all traces would quickly disappear. On came the Romans, undoubtedly outnumbering the Britons by about two to one; but as they reached the second rampart the hail of slingstones, a principal British weapon, would have become unendurable. At this point they formed a 'testudo', the Roman word for a tortoise. The testudo was made by each legionary holding his shield horizontally above his head and advancing in close-packed formation. A testudo was tested by having horsemen ride over it. This human tortoise with its impenetrable shell would be too much for the Britons who, seeing their principle weapon made ineffective, could suffer a loss of morale which even Caradoc could not restore. As the Romans came to close quarters they inflicted tremendous slaughter with their short swords. The prize they wanted, preferably alive, was Caradoc, but this they failed to achieve. The guerrilla leader fled from the field of battle, hoping to fight another day. In a mood of over-confidence he had allowed his wife and daughters to be present at the battle- perhaps in that matriarchal society he could not have pre-vented it-and they fell into Roman hands. He himself fled and took refuge with Cartimandua, Queen of the Brigantes. Alas for hopes. He was bound in chains and handed over to Ostorius. Doubtless he had hoped to incite the Brigantes to further rebellion against the Romans but he was seemingly unaware of the deviousness of Cartimandua, a lady of uncertain loyalties and varied love affairs. Thus Caradoc, captured by treachery, came to be exhibited as a captive in Rome.

Caradoc was a great guerrilla leader. Others would follow in his footsteps, with varying fortunes. He lived and fought so long ago that his remarkable abilities have been obscured. Perhaps the greatest tribute to Caradoc is the value the Romans set on his capture. They realized that he was not merely a great guerrilla fighter but was also a symbol of national unity. The names of Wallace, Boadicea, Alfred and Glyndwr are familiar to most people. Caradoc was the equal, perhaps the superior, of all. He should not be forgotten.

The capture of Caradoc did not end the battle for Wales. Undoubtedly it was a blow for the Britons but they fought back. The mantle of Caradoc was taken up by the Silures. Unfortunately we do not know the names of any of their leaders but their quality must have been remarkable. Ostorius soon received a rude shock. Under the impression that Welsh resistance was now crushed, he ordered the building of a series of border forts which would enable the Romans to control the Silures until such time as they (the Romans) decided to annex a further piece of Welsh territory.

But the Silures had other plans. First they attacked one of the border forts and killed most of its inhabitants. This fort has never been properly identified but it is suggested it may have been Clyro, which is a day's march from Kenchester, which is in turn a day's march from Hereford. However, it might equally have been Pen y Gaer, west of Gobannium (Abergavenny). However, all these forts were soon well aware that they were surrounded by hostile territory. Roman forts were built on an orthodox pattern and it was possible for an experienced observer to tell in a glance at the size and type of a fort how many men were inside. As we know from the experience of medieval soldiers over a thousand years later, you needed a very high wall to keep out the Welsh. There is no reason to suppose that the Silures were any less agile than their descendants who gave the Normans such a rough handling later.

But there was worse to come. In an engagement of which we have only the barest details, the Romans suffered the sort of reverse which Caradoc had wished to inflict. A Roman column was ambushed and scattered. Cavalry reinforcements which were rushed to the spot fared no better. Infantry was now fed in piecemeal as it came up, but to no avail. Finally, two entire legions were flung in and the position was held. At this point, with a feeling of a task well done, the jubilant Silures faded away into the woods. Clearly this battle must have taken place close to the main base at Gloucester for the legions to be brought in. It sounds like a day of bitter fighting, with the Romans committing perhaps 12,000 troops, and losing a good number in the process. This was ominous in the extreme and it is clear from Tacitus that it was no isolated threat. The Silures knew how to fight the Romans and it was not in pitched battles like that which sealed the fate of Caradoc but in sudden swift attacks, luring and ambushing. So continuous did these guerrilla attacks become that the Romans found themselves unable to move except in parties of considerable strength; it also strictly limited the routes they took. Anyone travelling in the area west of Gloucester today can well appreciate the Roman problem-and that after nearly two thousand years of tree-felling and land clearance. Ostorius raged and fumed, threatened to exterminate the Silures altogether and instructed his troops to use the utmost ruthlessness against his wily and infuriating opponents. Even so, matters went from bad to worse. Two Roman units, overbold and insufficiently cautious, were wiped out. Roman soldiers were captured and sent to various parts of Wales as slaves. It was all too much for Ostorius who such a short time before had been celebrating the capture of Caradoc and the presumed capitulation of the rest of Wales.

Ostorius died suddenly, though not in battle. The Silures celebrated the occasion by defeating yet another legion. These were major triumphs. This was not the occasional ambush of a handful of unimportant men; this was the continuous defeat of Roman forces, beleaguering them in their forts and defeating the legions sent to raise the siege. This time it was the 20th legion which had suffered – a crack unit of 5000 men.

Ostorius was succeeded by Didius Gallus in AD 52 and Didius was of a somewhat different type from his predecessor. Ostorius was essentially a field commander; Didius was no novice as a soldier but he added to his military expertise a nice sense of diplomacy.

He certainly needed all the cunning he could muster. Plans for the conquest of the Silures had not merely been postponed; they had become a branch of mythology. All along the Severn the Roman frontier was under threat. A rising else-where-and there would be two-could jeopardize the entire Roman army in Britain. When all this was reported in Rome there was some very serious thinking. Should Britain be abandoned? With many Romans the conquest of this ultima thule had never been welcome. It seemed to some almost profane to cross the Channel and venture into this dangerous country. The Romans knew their limitations; they could not go on expanding for ever. However, in AD 57 Nero, advised no doubt by his Higher Command, decided that the efforts put into Britain previously must not be wasted. The decision was given: all Britain would be conquered, including Wales.

By some means Didius had stabilized the frontier with Wales. How he did so is not known but it is suspected that he established marching camps and minor forts at such short intervals that Silures raiding parties were unable to penetrate without themselves being ambushed. It was not the way the Romans liked to conduct their military affairs but at that moment there was no choice.

In AD 57 Roman policy once more turned to conquest. First Veranius was sent to Britain but he died almost immediately; then Suetonius Paulinus. The latter was well-equipped for warfare in the Welsh countryside; instead of the heavy legionary who was ideal for the shock and struggle of pitched battle he mustered a force of lightly-armed soldiers who could cross mountain and stream with the same agility as the natives they were attacking. Whether Didius's diplomacy had softened up the Silures or whether their great, though unknown, guerrilla leaders were now dead is not known: perhaps both factors applied. Within three years Paulinus had conquered south Wales and had moved on to the north-west. In AD 60 he crossed the Menai Straits in flat-bottomed boats, defeated an army which included priests and women, and laid the foundations of a fort.

At that moment Boadicea (Boudicca) brought out the Iceni in revolt. A combination of brutality and stupidity by the Romans had made the rising inevitable. Colchester was overwhelmed and burnt and London suffered a similar fate. Suetonius hurried back from Anglesey. At some unrecorded spot – conjectured at being either at Mancetter, near Atherstone on the Watling Street, or Bagshot in Surrey – he fell on the Iceni who were now affected by weariness, loot and dissipation. It was the end of the rebellion.

But the Romans had not heard the last of the Silures, nor the Ordovices either. In ad 79 Frontinus had to mount a full scale campaign against the Silures and in the same year Agricola had to drive through the Ordovices' territory to Anglesey. Although the Romans were operating from a more secure base and had much experience to draw on, their task was far from easy. Only after years of establishing camps and forts, and linking them with roads, did the area seem to approach stability. The story of Roman warfare in Wales is recorded in the numerous roads, forts, marching camps and towns they built there. No better tribute to Welsh martial spirit can be found than the Roman town at Caerleon-on-Usk (Isca) near Newport. It was the headquarters of the Second Augusta Legion and it could accommodate 6000 legionaries. It is beautifully preserved and the visitor may walk through the barrack blocks and the amphitheatre. There is also an interesting museum with a replica of a fully-armed soldier.

Wales is a small country but its fighting men have had stout hearts. Every conqueror has unwittingly left a tribute to Welsh tenacity: the Romans by their fortresses of which Caerleon is a fine example, the Normans by their mottes, and the Plantagenets by the great Edwardian castles. The Welsh do not resent any of them; they are justly proud of them as a tribute to their ancestors.

Chapter 3

THE BATTLES FOR SUPREMACY

In the previous chapter we spoke of the tremendous battle the legionaries fought in order to conquer Wales. As a result the Romans succeeded in occupying the valleys and plains; the mountainous areas were left largely to the Britons. What is known as 'Wild Wales' has defied successive attempts to conquer it. On occasions armies have penetrated its most remote and difficult regions but when the campaign was over the local people once more took possession. After the battles in the first century AD Roman relations with the Welsh took a course which they could not have predicted. In some areas such as the south and north-west they established good relations with the local people. There was mutual respect for the fighting qualities of former opponents and the Welsh were so favourably impressed with the culture of the invaders that they quickly adopted it. As with the rest of Britain – though to a lesser extent – this acceptance of Roman suzerainty eventually brought them near to disaster. The enervating influence of peace and the presence of Roman legions made the British forget their own martial skills. Thus when the Romans withdrew at the end of the fourth century the British were so accustomed to the relaxing effect of peace that at first they were easy prey. This effect was more clearly marked in the south-east of Britain than in the west and north, but to some extent it existed everywhere.

There were, of course, Welsh who had joined the Roman legions. The benefit of this to the recruit was that he knew that in the course of time he would become a Roman citizen and be granted a piece of land. The benefits to Rome were obvious in that it enabled them to colonize territories with reliable veterans who had often been induced to enlist by this form of social security. There was, however, a considerable disadvantage to the territory from which the recruits were drawn. Its more adventurous young men were drawn into the Roman army and perhaps posted to another area, Hadrian's Wall, the German frontier, or Gaul or Spain, and the recruiting area was policed by a legion whose members often came from a distant territory. When Rome was in decline and the legions were withdrawn to defend the capital, the outlying territories of the Roman empire – such as Wales – found they had been almost denuded of potential warriors.

Furthermore, as the Romans had been quick to note, the peoples of Wales showed an enduring resistance to any moves for unity. Apart from the larger groupings there was intense enmity between one family and another; there was an even more striking division between north and south. With considerable wisdom the Romans had made every effort to stamp out Druidism. Although in general the Romans interfered little with the religion of conquered territories they behaved otherwise in Wales. Ostensibly their reason was the revulsion which the Druidical custom of human sacrifice aroused in them; in practice it was probably the memory of the fanaticism displayed by the Welsh at the time of Caradoc and Suetonius. The army which had confronted the latter on Anglesey was enough to strike terror in any soldier's heart. Between the Welsh ranks were priests calling down curses on the invading army, and dashing here and there were women whose black clothing, long, streaming, dishevelled hair, and flaming torches, made them seem more like fiends than humans. However, apart from the intimidating and spectacular side of their religion, the Druids had other qualities which made them a threat to an invader, qualities which have been obscured in the mythology which has subsequently grown up around them. The Druids represented the best of Celtic intellectual and cultural tradition. They were the repositories of information and the dispensers of knowledge. If anyone was able to unite the whole of Wales it was the Druids. In Anglesey they had control of valuable food supplies-not for nothing is that island known as 'the granary of Wales'. They knew how to appeal to the more intelligent of the peoples of Wales and how to mystify, dazzle and incite the more primitive. The Roman decision to eradicate the influence of the Druids was undoubtedly a shrewd one.

Even after the elimination of the Druids the Romans treated Welsh military potential with respect. A fully equipped legion was stationed at each end of the frontier-at Chester and Caerleon, and the forts which were now dotted along the pattern of strategic roads were kept fully manned. Wales was valuable to the Romans as a source of economic and strategic materials. The mines produced copper, lead, iron, coal and, not least, gold. There was a prosperous working at Dolaucothi in Dyfed (665 404). This is conveniently close to the A482. The Romans had arranged two aqueducts here for gold-washing. Pumpsaint has been excavated and yielded interesting material. Visitors who wish to explore the area may obtain leaflets from the Cothi Arms. The gold was not worked out in Roman times so there are medieval workings here also, and a Norman motte. Although this seems a relatively small and unimportant area it was not considered so by the Romans. Gold is one of the sinews of war!

Until recently it was thought that Caerwent was the principal Roman town. Excavations prove that Carmarthen was as important and had its own amphitheatre.

By the third century the Welsh saw the Romans as allies rather than overlords; a century later, when the Roman armies had withdrawn, there were families of Roman stock who chose to continue to live in Wales rather than return to their original homelands. From these latter some modern Welsh names are derived. Emrys and Rhys are derivatives of Ambrosius which in Latin meant the equivalent of 'immortal'; Owen comes from Eugenius.

The Romans were effectively in Wales for three hundred years. It was a long time and it is not surprising that the two peoples formed close links. In that time Rome passed from being an empire at the height of its power to a nation in decline. Decline, in fact, began soon after the peak of power; the end was rapid and chaotic. Rome was not so much destroyed from without as destroyed from within: self-seeking generals, corruption and debauchery produced lassitude and inept direction at a time when the Roman empire had most need of the efficient use of its resources.

The effects of this were felt in Britain in the third century AD. The southern coast of the country began to experience raids from Saxon invaders whose policy seemed merely to destroy. The Roman counter to them was to build a chain of forts along the southern coast of Britain and appoint a Count of the Saxon Shore', who also commanded a defensive fleet. Substantial remains of the forts may be seen today, notably at Pevensey, Sussex, Portchester, Hampshire, and Dover, Kent. The Roman fort at Cardiff was undoubtedly strengthened at this time. Its outer walls have been excavated and are on view to visitors; they were built into the later fortifications but are now uncovered.

But the Saxons were not the only enemy threatening Britain at this time. Up in the north the people known as Picts were a constant threat. Attempts were made to keep them out by building three different walls, of which Hadrian's is the most famous; all failed eventually.

Wales had a problem all of its own but no less difficult. From the third century the whole of the western seaboard of Wales was under intermittent but continuous attack from the Irish. They were, at that time, called Scots and some of them later moved into Scotland and gave their name to the whole of that country. They too were Celts but they felt little common ground with the people of Wales. It was the Irish threat as much as the Saxon one which caused the strengthening of Cardiff, for the Irish raiders sailed up the Severn on numerous destructive occasions. Even more vulnerable was Anglesey, which produced copper as well as grain, and a strong fort was built at Holyhead to safeguard it. By the fourth century Roman-occupied Britain presented a very different picture from that of the first century. Many high Roman officials were not of Roman stock at all; they were Teutonic or Gallic or Spanish. Undoubtedly these were responsible for certain policy changes and contradictions; in one area fighting against die invaders might be as bitter as ever, yet in another a party of foreigners would be invited to settle and form a minor buffer state. Some of the Irish settled in the western parts of Dyfed.

In AD 287 it seemed as though Britain might find a new role but the phase was short-lived. Carausius, the Count of the Saxon Shore, had proclaimed himself Emperor and independent of Rome. He was entirely successful in his activities: he held off Pict and Scot and chased the Saxon marauders off the scene. But after seven years Carausius was murdered and Britain was once more reunited to Rome. Even so, events continued to go well for Britain. The emperors Constantius and Constantine both spent much time here.

The years 383-8 produced another remarkable emperor, and one with distinctly Welsh associations. This was Macsen Wledig, a Spaniard in Roman service whose imperial name was Magnus Maximus (the great greatest). Macsen had shown great skill at arms against the Picts and Scots and left Britain in 383 to stake his claim to the imperial diadem. He shared his supreme power with two other aspirants, Theodosius and Valentinian II, but overreached himself and was executed in 388. Macsen Wledig is a particularly interesting character because he married Elen of Caernarvon. One of his daughters married Vortigem, King of south-east England. (Vortigem was the king who unwisely invited the Jutes Hengist and Horsa to help him against the Saxons but found them unwilling to leave subsequently.) Later Kings of Dyfed and Powys claimed descent from Macsen.

Claims of direct descent from illustrious personages who lived before the age of recorded pedigrees must be regarded with some scepticism; indirect descent is another matter and in a small community with constant intermarriage, over a long period every single person eventually has some tie of kinship with illustrious antecedents.

Macsen's great achievement for Wales was not so much that he established dynasties as that he stabilized the country, rekindled a spirit of national unity, and firmly established the basis of the Christian religion. Wales, of course, did not become a whole-heartedly Christian community overnight but Macsen's encouragement, combined with the activities of monks and missionaries, laid the foundation for the religious fervour which has characterized Wales over the centuries. But the greatest impetus came from St David, the Patron Saint of Wales. His lifetime (520-90) spanned most of the sixth century, a crucial time for Wales. He encouraged the founding of monasteries and preached the virtues of simplicity and frugality. Perhaps his austere diet was mainly composed of leeks, which have, for some unknown reason, become the Welsh emblem. One feels there is a touch of humour about the adoption of this useful but unpretentious vegetable as a national symbol. It is, however, more nutritious than a rose, a thistle, a lily or a maple leaf.

After the Romans left Wales we are in the period which has aptly been described as the Dark Ages. We know that there were pagan settlers from Ireland in Dyfed at this time because archaeologists have found inscriptions made by them on stone, and there are a few place names which date from this period. However, most of our knowledge of personalities and events is a compound legend and imaginative reconstruction. Cunedda is an example of a tantalizing character who clearly existed and did much for Wales, but of whom little is known. It is said he was a Pict from Scotland who came to Wales in the fifth century and established a dynasty in Gwynedd. There is only one place which bears his name – Altt Cunedda – but his son Ceredig gave his name to Ceredigion (Cardigan). Cunedda made Deganwy, opposite Llandudno, into a stronghold. Cunedda is said to be the ancestor of all the Kings of north Wales, including the famous Llywelyns.

Another notable character was Maelgwn who was the dominant king in north Wales in the sixth century. His headquarters was apparently Deganwy. Anglesey represented the western limit of his kingdom until he decided that the whole of western Wales should be under his authority. The Celtic frontiers were at this time coming under pressure from the advancing Saxons, but it is doubtful whether Maelgwn took this fact into his calculations. One of his assets appears to have been a fleet based on Anglesey, and with the aid of this and some land expeditions he was able to summon the minor princelings of the west coast of Wales to a 'conference' at Aberdovey at which his formal supremacy as King of all Wales should be recognized. Possession of such a centrally strategic spot must have added considerable force to his argument but persuasion was also reinforced by a melodramatic contest. The story is that it was agreed that the man who could sit longest in his chair in spite of the rising tide should be monarch over all. Maelgwn had taken the precaution to have a special chair with suitable wax floats and when the other chairs were knocked over by the tide this succeeded in floating.

This may seem to many a legend of fantasy if not absurdity but there are interesting undertones to it. This sort of command over the elements is a familiar theme in the mystique of regal appointments. The successful candidate appears to produce a much-needed shower of rain or perhaps show un-usual luck in surviving a flash of lightning which kills his rivals. Defeating the vagaries of the tide, which is by no means consistent as we know from Biblical and later history, adds greatly to prestige. The Canute legend of his telling the tide to retreat is believed by some to refer to unsuccessful attempts at land reclamation in eastern England; it seems not unlikely that the Maelgwn story found its way across England and was eventually, in garbled form, attributed to Canute. Owing to the vagueness of many early legends there has been a tendency among historians to dismiss whole centuries of alleged chronicles as superstitious legend. Some of these material, no-nonsense critics have had a sharp knock to their self-confidence in recent years when archaeologists and others, often by accident, have discovered relics which support some of the ancient legends. Dinas Emrys, near Beddgelert, is one of these sites. Future excavations may well discover others and it is clearly as unwise to be too sceptical of legend as it is to be too credulous.

Maelgwn was a Christian, although for most of his life one of name rather than deed. At one point he retired to a monastery but later reappeared to become even more of a tyrant than before. He died of what is described as 'yellow plague', a contagious disease which was sweeping the country at the time.

Elsewhere there were two battles which profoundly affected the future of Wales, but as neither could be said to have taken place in Wales they have been described elsewhere in this series (Famous Battles of the Midlands). The first was the battle of Mount Badon in 516. Badon has been attributed to various sites, but there is no genuine reason for supposing it need have been anywhere other than at the village of Baydon in Wiltshire finishing on the nearby Liddington Castle, an Iron Age fort on a 900-foot hill. The battle represented a major defeat for the Saxons who were blithely pushing westward, having overwhelmed much of southern England. Their crushing defeat at Baydon set back their conquest of the west by some fifty years. The architect of British victory appears to have been a man of Roman descent whose hill name was Ambrosius Aurelianus; his parents were Roman aristocrats who had settled in Britain and been massacred by the Saxons. Ambrosius had dedicated his life to being a guerrilla fighter and harassing the Saxons. He may well have been the legendary King Arthur, being known variously as Ambrosius, Aurelianus, Artos (the Celtic word for bear) – mere speculation of course. Ambrosius's connection with the Arthurian legend is supported by the fact that Celtic Britons at this time occupied not merely Wales but also Cornwall. Tintagel, in particular, and Cornwall in general are very closely associated with Arthur, as is also Glastonbury in Somerset. So too is Cadbury in Wiltshire. After the defeat of the Saxons these would have been the perimeter of Arthur's kingdom.

The second decisive battle of the sixth century was at Dyrham (originally Deorham) in Gloucestershire, in AD 577. On this occasion the Britons were less fortunate, and were decisively defeated. It was a disastrous occasion for it enabled the Saxons to break through and reach the Severn, thus separating the Britons of Wales from the Britons of Somerset, Devon and Cornwall. This strategic leap forward by the invaders was soon to be followed by an equally decisive battle at Chester in 613. It was, in fact, a victory won by Aethelfrith, King of Bernicia, but it had the far-reaching effect of cutting off the Britons of Wales from their fellows whose territories extended through Lancastria and Cumbria up to Strathclyde.

But before leaving the sixth century we should mention the remarkable achievement of the Britons in colonizing Brittany. The 'colonization' was rather different from what was later understood by the term for it was the result of St Teilo and a small party travelling to Brittany to escape the yellow plague to which we referred earlier. They were the first of many visitors and settlers to that country and the visitor to Brittany today will not fail to note the number of Celtic place-names, nor the fact that the Welsh language is closely akin to Breton. The Bretons will draw attention to this kinship. Curiously enough, the Welsh colonization of Brittany was partly the reverse process of what had happened a thousand years earlier in the Iron Age.

During this century, but probably for a long time before, and certainly after, a curious transformation was happening to the Welsh language. The stages and reasons are obscure. By the sixth century there was already a distinction – though not a great one-between the Brythonic (British) Celtic of north Wales and Goidelic or Gaelic spoken in Ireland. There were, and of course are, dialectic variations in most languages and someone who has gone to considerable trouble to learn the language and thus comprehend a culture may find himself baffled on occasion by words, phrases or intonations which are entirely local. However, the changes which took place in the Welsh language during the sixth century and after have never been adequately explained. The Celts living in north Wales spoke of Caratacus – the form heard by the Romans who recorded it as Caratacos. Later Caratacos became shortened to Caratoc, the 't' softened into a 'd' and in some parts the final 'c' became 'g', giving the word 'Caradog'. The same sort of transformation occurred in many other words. Although there are said to be no traces – apart from one or two place names – of the Irish who invaded and settled in Dyfed at this time, there seems a possibility that their version of Celtic (i.e. Goidelic or Gaelic) blended with Brythonic to produce what became known as Welsh rather than Celtic. Needless to say the language did not stand still and variations occurred in each century. Old Welsh may be encountered in literary works. The arrival of Henry VII on the English throne in 1485 did nothing but harm to the Welsh language; the English found Welsh so inconvenient to understand that in 1536 in the Act of Union it ceased to be an official language. Nevertheless the continuation of Welsh was ensured by the Welsh translation of the Bible in 1588 and the widespread use of that Bible in the eighteenth century by the Methodists.

Today Welsh is mainly preserved in the western districts but of a population of 2f million in Wales only half a million speak it. Fifty years ago nearly 300,000 people spoke Welsh alone; today it is unlikely that any Welsh speaker cannot speak English too when he wishes. But Welsh is not entirely confined to Wales. There are 8000 Welsh speakers in Patagonia, descendants of the people who went there from Wales in 186$ to settle and colonize.

The battle of Chester in 613, which we briefly referred to above, long remained in men's memories on account of subsequent atrocities. The objectives of Aethelfrith do not appear to have been strategic, for he made little use of his victory. Aethelfrith's rule extended from the Tyne to the Humber and was separated from the Celtic kingdoms by the Pen- nines. However, the battle of Chester was probably the result of restless ambition rather than any rational policy. Aethelfrith had previously conquered his neighbour the King of Deira (south Yorkshire) and had also gained a crushing victory over the Scots somewhere in the area of Liddesdale. When he came to Chester the Britons decided that all available force must be mustered against him and, recalling the morale-boosting efforts of the Druid priests in earlier wars, decided on this occasion to summon Christian priests to the battlefield. The British leader was Brocmail, of whom we know nothing more than the fact that he was their leader and he escaped from the battlefield with a mere fifty men. The two hundred Christian priests were massacred. Aethelfrith considered that even if they did not use weapons they used prayers and therefore could not claim to be non-combatants. It is a sad fact of history that when there is a religious factor involved in any battle the conflict tends to become more ruthless.

The effect of the battle was to drive the Britons from the Chester area. The city became deserted but a number of Angles soon settled in the neighbourhood. From these there may have been other incursions into north Wales, where there are – or were until recently – traces of battlefields. One of these, Maes Garmon, near Mold, is believed to date from an earlier period, that is ad 420. Although many bones were found here the monument was not erected till 1736 and the alleged combatants, the Britons under two bishops with the Latin names of Lupus and Germanus and the Saxons, whose commander's name is unknown, could scarcely have met as early as the fifth century. The authority for the battle is Bede but his account does not tally with the existence of bones in mass graves. According to his description, the Britons lay in ambush position and as the enemy came up the two bishops showed themselves. They shouted 'Alleluia' three times. The 'Alleluia' was taken up by the Britons in hiding and the invaders were so disconcerted at this reception that they fled, throwing away their arms as they went. It is possible that the Venerable Bede did not know the full story but only as much of it as was considered suitable for ecclesiastical ears.

Mold had another interesting relic of former times but this, like so many similar discoveries, disappeared soon after it was discovered in the early nineteenth century. This was at a place called Bryn-yi Ellyllon (fairy hill). Under a large cairn of stones which was removed for roadmaking and building there was discovered a skeleton wearing armour of bronze and gold. There were also amber beads and remains of iron weapons in the tomb.

The juxtaposition of military and religious memorials is very close in this area. Of Denbigh, Rhuddlan and Flint we shall have more to say later. These were places for strife and death and wounds. Holywell, in contrast, was a place for healing and it preserved this reputation for many centuries. Nowadays, most healing waters have been chemically analysed and pronounced to be of no special value. However, scientific medicine, like scientific agriculture, is now beginning to doubt its own infallibility and to speculate whether some of the folk lore of the past may not have had more benefits to it than was recently thought. Even so, the supposed origin of the Holywell benefit requires rather more credulity than one can reasonably expect. In the seventh century a virtuous maiden called Winefrede caught the eye of a ruthless prince called Cradocus. Enraged at having his attentions rebuffed, Cradocus ran after her one day and cut off her head with a sweep of his sword. Divine retribution was swift. The earth opened up and swallowed Cradocus. The head rolled down the hill and stopped close by the church. Where it stopped a spring began to flow and has never ceased. Its water had remarkable healing powers whose fame soon spread far and wide.

But that was not the end of Winefrede. A well-known saint, St Bueno, came by, saw the head and picked it up. He carried it to the bleeding trunk, fitted it in place, prayed, and there was Winefrede alive and well. She lived for fifteen years and in that time founded a nunnery.

However, the seventh century has left records of other and less elevating events than the life and adventures of Winefrede. Aethelfrith, King of Northumbria, died soon after defeating the Welsh at the battle of Chester (613) and was succeeded by Eadwine, an even more warlike figure. Although officially a Christian, Eadwine had a somewhat simplistic view of his newly-adopted faith. Provided it brought him victory in battle he was perfectly ready to be baptized and call himself a Christian. He had no cause for complaint. This Christian soldier ravaged the land from Scotland to Essex and even built a fleet which conquered the Isle of Man and Anglesey.

Inevitably this degree of power produced a coalition of those who felt that their lands would be the next to fall to the warlike northener. The King of Gwynedd at this time was Cadwallon, and after seeing the fate of Anglesey he had no hesitation in allying himself with Penda, King of Mercia (the English Midlands). Penda, in fact, was a fervent anti- Christian, so this was an alliance of a Christian and a heathen against a Christian. The rival forces met on an unknown battlefield near Doncaster, called, somewhat vaguely, Heathfield, in 632. Eadwine was killed in scenes of great carnage.

Cadwallon advanced to York, which he captured. For a time it seemed as if the pendulum had swung back and the Britons might once again dominate the whole island. But it was not to be so. Cadwallon was killed fighting near the Great Wall in 635 on the battlefield of Heavenfield. His conqueror was Oswald, a son of the dead Eadwine. At this time Cadwallon was still in alliance with Penda and the Mercians but soon the former allies were to become bitter enemies. Cadwallon was succeeded by his son Cadwallader. At this moment the fortunes of Wales which so recently had seemed promising appeared to be in rapid decline.

Oswald drove Cadwallader and Penda out of Northumbria and pressed on towards Wales. However, he was intercepted near Oswestry in 643 and killed by Penda. It is said that the town takes its name from a tree under which Oswald was buried (Oswald's tree); and this too was said to possess miraculous healing powers. There is an Iron Age fort at Oswestry and it could well have been the site of the battle. Oswestry is a long way from Northumbria and dangerously close to the heart of Wales. Unfortunately for Wales Oswald was succeeded by his brother Oswiu, who was even more of a warrior. Oswiu disposed of the aged though still vigorous Penda at Winwaedfeld, a battlefield thought to be in south Yorkshire. Penda was 80 at the time. Oswiu then became the Bretwalda, the title held by the supreme king in Britain. It was the end of Welsh and Mercian aspirations in the north and soon we find the other kingdoms, including Wales, paying tribute to the great Northumbrian. This did not prevent yet another struggle for power beginning: between Wales and Mercia. Unfortunately for Wales, Mercian power was rapidly in the ascendant. Three able kings – Aethelred, Aethelbald and Offa – ruled Mercia for over a century between them and the last of these had the greatest effect on Wales. Offa, in fact, was well known outside the British Isles. His most valuable contribution to history is the famous Offa's Dyke, a ditch which runs from Chepstow in the south to a point two miles short of Prestatyn in the north. It is a favourite haunt of walkers for it is easily accessible, presents no difficulties and goes through extremely beautiful scenery. The fact that it ends two miles short of the northern coast is probably explained by the fact that Offa himself is believed to have been killed near Rhuddlan. It seems probable that the Welsh were determined that the dyke should never be completed and Offa took the army into north Wales to ensure that it was. Clearly he failed in this last task.

But the rest of the dyke is nothing short of miraculous. The actual frontier between Wales and Mercia some 1200 years ago was 150 miles long. Offa's Dyke covered 80 miles of this for there were some stretches which, because of rivers and ravines, did not need defending. It may easily be explored because, in 1971, after many years of negotiations over rights of way, the path was officially opened. The walker may now walk along 176 miles of path, or a lesser distance if he so desires. As a frontier and barrier he may not find the dyke itself very impressive, for the ditch does not look very deep nor the bank very high. However, when lined with armed men it was probably a very satisfactory boundary marker. If you walk 17 miles a day, which some people think is a suitable distance, you will cover the path in ten days but in doing so you will miss many places deserving of closer investigation, such as Whitecastle in Gwent; it is not a walk to hurry over. Like all earthworks the dyke was undoubtedly more formidable at the time of its construction than after centuries of weathering and is a major feat not merely of engineering but of motivation too. There are laconic records in the chronicles which refer to victories won by Offa at this time, one in 776 in south Wales and another in 780 also 'against the Britons'. The Britons might well have resisted Offa as best they could. The area which is now Shropshire was a form of no-man's-land which was mainly occupied by Britons. The principal town in the area was Pengwem which later acquired the name of Shrewsbury. Offa's campaign put Pengwem clearly on his side of the dyke.

But Offa was not the only enemy with which Wales had to contend at this time. Raiders began to appear along the west coast. They were the dreaded Norsemen whose swift brutal raids would soon extend to the whole coastline of Britain and, at times, penetrate far inland. An even more dangerous and continuing enemy was dissension from within. Wales had never been united but now the country was moving into times when national solidarity was vital. Now alas, Wales was torn by the fratricidal rivalry between Conan and Howel, twin sons of Rhodri Molwynog. They abandoned the minor princelings to the fate of being conquered by Offa and fought a relentless battle for the ownership of Anglesey. After Offa's death matters deteriorated even further. The Mercian king was succeeded by Cenwulf who pushed right through south Wales to Dyfed and even burnt Deganwy, near Conway in the north. Welsh fortunes now seemed at their lowest ebb.

But the darkest hour comes before the dawn, philosophic-ally if not in actual fact. Conan died in 815 and his brother soon after; their successors were less vindictive but quite incapable of creating a Welsh renaissance. But, in 844, came Rhodri the Great. At the same time Mercian power began to decline and Wessex, further removed from Wales, became the dominant British power. Rhodri, who was killed in 876, spent most of his life fighting the Norsemen, although he had other bitter and strenuous encounters with the men of Mercia and Wessex. In the early years of his reign he had a great victory over his Norse enemies (who were known by the Welsh as 'the black pagans') at Llandudno. The Norse leader, Horm, was killed and the event is commemorated by the name of the mountain there, Great Orme. However, the battle in which Rhodri met his death was against the Mercians and it seems that he must have temporarily allied himself to a Danish force at that time. Rhodri's career has something in common with that of Alfred. Both had to go into hiding for a while and both emerged to fight more battles. Rhodri's contribution to Welsh power was perhaps not so much his personal victories but the fact that he left six warlike sons, who fought against outsiders rather than between themselves. A further contribution to the unity of Wales was provided by Howel Dda, King of Dyfed. Howel codified the laws of Wales, a stupendous task in view of the diversity of local customs. However, codifying the laws is one thing, enforcing them is another. In the years after Howel's death Wales lived in a state of anarchy. The counoy was ravaged by Norsemen along the coast and by English along the eastern borders. The Welsh retreated into the valleys and defended themselves as best they could.

Revival came under Llywelyn ap Seisyll who defeated an ambitious Prince of Deheubarth at Aber Gwii, in Towy, and established himself as King of Wales. For a time there was peace but in 1022 when Llywelyn died all the minor prince-lings declared their independence. Anarchy reigned once more and Llywelyn's son, Griffith ap Llywelyn, had to flee to Ireland.

For sixteen years all was chaos and destruction in Wales once more. But then Griffith ap Llywelyn returned. The methods by which he assembled his armies are not known. All we know definitely is that within a year he had defeated a powerful Mercian army at Rhyd y Groes on the Severn and followed this by two victories against rivals, the first at Pencader in 1041 to give him control over Cardigan, and the second near Newport in 1044, to give him control of south-east Wales.

The same year Harold, later to be the King of England and defeated at the Battle of Hastings, became Earl of Wessex. It was clear to Griffith that an extension of Welsh power over the Severn would rapidly bring him into conflict with this vigorous Saxon. Harold's military reputation has suffered from his defeat at Hastings, but in the 22 years before that date it was eclipsed by no one. 1055 was a decisive year for Griffith. Wessex and Mercia quarrelled over the earldom of the latter, which went to Harold's brother. The deposed Earl of Mercia fled to Wales where, in spite of ancient enmities, a treaty was concluded, and Griffith married the Mercian's daughter.

Acting on the principle that the attacker has everything in his favour, Griffith marched briskly into Herefordshire, brushing on one side the indifferent army which had been hastily assembled to keep him out. Thus far everything went according to plan. Harold appeared to accept the news with philosophic resignation; he certainly had enough problems elsewhere. His realm stretched as far north as Scotland where he had recently organized the defeat of Macbeth and succession of Malcolm. However, the Marches were not entirely quiet for the Bishop of Hereford assembled a mixed force of Norman and English. There were already a few Norman settlers in England at this time, favourites of Edward the Confessor, and they had built a few castles and made themselves obnoxious to the local people. The fact that Leofgar was a bishop did not prevent him from being a military man. Bishops at this time and later were often extremely warlike. Ecclesiastical law forbade them to carry swords but instead they carried a murderous mace which was probably more effective. However, Leofgar did not get very far. Griffith intercepted him soon after he had crossed the dyke, scattered his army and killed the bishop.

However, Harold was merely biding his time. It was a pity that he and Griffith were such implacable enemies for they would have made a fine combination. Harold knew very well that to march a conventional Saxon army into Wales was merely requesting a crushing defeat. Instead he trained an army which could cross rivers and climb mountains. He could draw on all comers of England, and parts of Scotland, for his recruits, so the army, when it marched, was the best available and well-suited for its purpose. Harold, being well aware of potential as well as actual dissensions in the Welsh ranks, sent in agents with tempting offers.

This process took a considerable time. Eight years later Harold was ready to move. He proceeded to act with a bewildering series of switch attacks. First he concentrated his forces at Gloucester as if to launch an attack on south Wales. He had already based a fleet at Bristol and this was making intimidatory swoops along the coast. Suddenly he marched north: Harold was an expert at these long unexpected marches as was later shown before the battle of Stamford Bridge. Griffith, expecting an attack from the south, suddenly found himself hard pressed in the north. Harold's men penetrated the valleys separating Griffith's allies from each other. Even worse was the fact that Griffith scarcely knew whom to trust. The divisions within Wales, the product of long years of bitterness and strife, were clearly only patched over. There was a reward of 300 cattle for Griffith's head. When the Welsh king had been driven back to the higher crags of Snowdon it was not the enemy but his own men who killed him. His head was cut off and taken to Harold. Harold thereupon married Griffith's widow and appointed Griffith's brothers as regional commanders. It seems extraordinary to modem ears that widows should marry their husband's conquerors, and defeated kings should have their family placed in positions of greater authority than they had previously known, but this was by no means the only occasion on which it happened. Had Harold lived, Wales would have undoubtedly enjoyed peace and prosperity, but three years later Harold was killed at Hastings and Wales was laid open for the Norman invasions.

Chapter 4

THE BATTLES AGAINST THE NORMANS

The successes of the Normans all over Britain and not least in Wales owed much to the man they killed at Hastings. Harold had not only united the peoples of Wessex, Mercia, East Anglia and Northumbria, he had also pacified the Scottish and Welsh marches. Even more, in the week before his defeat and death he had destroyed the finest army ever to leave Scandinavia in the battle of Stamford Bridge. The Normans therefore were able to pursue the subjugation of their newly conquered lands without much hindrance. They brought a totally alien way of life, and harsh customs and laws. But at first they encountered little resistance.

They had, of course, brought in a totally different pattern of warfare, and soon Wales would bear traces of it. Until the Normans, warfare in Britain had been conducted by foot soldiers, some with bows but most with spears, swords or axes. Horses were used for transport but not in battle. Armour was usually a leather jerkin and occasionally an iron helmet. For a time the Saxons used throwing axes but these gradually fell into disuse as being an expensive and not over-effective weapon. Their troops were extremely mobile. When fighting in difficult terrain such as the Welsh mountains the Saxons discarded their long spears and heavy shields.

Norman weapons, armour and tactics were quite different. Campaign tactics were designed for the heavily armoured mounted knight. He had a pot-helmet, with a cover for the nose known as 'the nasal', a long chain-mail jerkin, a long triangular shield and heavy sword. Archers were present on the battlefield but the bows had a comparatively short range.

But these were the weapons of Norman tactics; the weapons of Norman strategy were even more effective. William the Conqueror's plan was to make his barons responsible for newly occupied lands. He did this by allotting huge estates while at the same time creating a triangle of responsibility. At the apex of the triangle was the baron and under the baron were various feudal dependants, each living in a manor. Each baron proceeded to build a very effective fortification at every strategic point in his new territory. These key points would be the entrances to valleys, the side of fords, the junction of rivers or roads, and the appropriate point for the surveillance of townships. The fortification was quickly erected by throwing up an earth mound and protecting it with a ditch at the base. On the top would be a wooden palisade. This was the simplest form of the motte and bailey castle. Soon it became more elaborate, ditches were widened into deep moats or even lakes, wood was replaced by stone, and a series of outer palisades made entrance to the citadel even more difficult. However, the essential point was that the motte or mound, 50-100 feet high, should have sides so steep that a horseman could not climb them. This technique of fortification had been widely used in Normandy. These primitive castles were of equal value in an attacking or a defensive strategy. A cluster of motte and bailey castles could mask the advance into enemy-held territory, giving the holder temporary immunity while he surveyed the land. Against an invader they were equally useful for it was a rash commander who would negligently march past these petty strongholds leaving them unsubdued and thus in an ideal position to cut his communications. However, if he stopped to reduce them he lost valuable time and wasted essential troops in an operation which might be lengthy, expensive and frustrating.

The castle holders chosen for the Welsh border were the Earls of Chester (Hugh the Wolf), Shrewsbury (Roger of Montgomery), and Hereford (William FitzOsbern). Their task was to hold the frontier and extend it into Wales wherever possible.

The arrival of the Normans saw the disappearance of many familiar place-names and the arrival of new ones. Wessex, Mercia, Northumbria were obliterated and instead the English countryside was divided into shires. In time these shires would penetrate into Wales and names like Radnorshire, Caernarvonshire and Pembrokeshire became a familiar part of the Welsh scene. In 1974 these names would be swept away in Wales and replaced by earlier ones – but not the earliest. Although the change was welcomed by local government administrators who saw them as 'reforms', the new names were not universally popular. They were disliked by tourists who found them too general and irritated many people who saw them as examples of bureaucratic interference with tradition.

Norman rule soon became hated. Nobody likes being conquered but some victors feel that their most fruitful policy will be to bear lightly on the defeated and to enlist their co-operation wherever possible. The Normans intended to obtain the co-operation of the defeated English, but there was no question of bearing lightly on them for that purpose. After they had parcelled out the land to powerful French-speaking barons, they set up a judicial system alien to English thought, and enforced it by a feudal military structure. Many of the judicial words in the English language today are Norman in origin, and in the years after the Norman Conquest everything Norman symbolized oppression.

Not surprisingly, this intense hatred of the new overlords soon showed itself in open revolt. William had returned to Normandy in 1067 and almost as soon as he had departed there was a widespread rebellion. Unfortunately for the rebels they gave each other no assistance and William, who had returned at once to England on hearing what was happening in his absence, was able to deal with the insurrection piecemeal. His campaigns against Exeter and Ely, and in the north, do not concern us here except for their results. His policy of deterrence was based not on reforms but on extreme terrorism. Exeter was the first to feel his cruelty but Yorkshire would remember it the longest. He slaughtered and burnt from the Humber to the Tees so devastatingly that the whole area remained waste for twenty years. The effect of this was to make the people of the Welsh marches more determined than ever but courage was not enough against Norman armour, and the revolt was crushed by 1070. Even while it was going on Wales had been torn by an internal struggle. Bleddyn, the brother of Griffith ap Llywelyn, fought a bitter battle at Mechen against Griffith's two sons; both were killed. This gave him control of Gwynedd and Powys.

He was unable to extend his domain any further south for that area was effectively controlled by Meredith ap Owen.

But William had chosen his border barons well. The Earl of Chester was soon probing westwards, first to Rhuddlan and later to Deganwy. There was no rest from the Normans. They were apparently only happy when fighting and the hardships of a campaign were a stimulus rather than a check to them. The Welsh were capable fighting men when the occasion demanded, but fighting was not their sole pre-occupation. By relentless pressure, pivoting their attack on one strong point after another, the Normans were able to drive deeply into the fertile parts of Wales. The mountains were a different matter and the Normans were careful not to put themselves in a position where their heavy equipment would leave them at a disadvantage against the lightly armed Welsh.

Shrewsbury, as we saw earlier in the book, was well placed for the launching of attacks into central Wales. It was the Earldom of Roger of Montgomery, who had provided sixty ships for the original invasion, and commanded the right wing in the Battle of Hastings. Roger was soon succeeded by his son, Robert of Belesme, who had a ruthless mother, Mabel of Belesme. Fortunately for all, Mabel was assassinated and Robert imprisoned for life after an unsuccessful rebellion against Henry I. Robert did however contribute something useful to posterity. He imported Spanish horses which formed the basis of a famous Powys Stud.

Meanwhile an even more effective pressure on Wales was coming from William FitzOsbern, Earl of Hereford. FitzOsbern soon pushed his frontier into Gwent and built a strong castle at Chepstow. Chepstow would be the scene of some memorable battles. The castle was probably begun as early as 1068, perhaps even earlier. Although the Normans made use of motte and bailey castles in all areas on certain occasions, if the material was readily available they built in stone. Chepstow was an example. FitzOsbern built an oblong castle of two storeys, with the entrance well above ground level. Although it has been altered slightly, it is substantially the same as when he built it on a bend in the Wye. (The castle is sometimes known as 'striguil', which means 'a bend in the river'.) Its siting was a good example of Norman strategic skill. It overlooked a harbour which could take supplies coming up from Bristol, it controlled the main road into south Wales and it was well-positioned to monitor any traffic up or down river. In subsequent years other buildings were placed around FitzOsbern's great Norman donjon, and Chepstow today is a mecca for tourists. FitzOsbern spent his life as an active warrior, and by a combination of courage, skill, and cunning managed to conquer most of Gwent before his death in 1071. His son Roger of Breteuil lacked his father's judgement. Roger did not feel much sense of feudal loyalty to William the Conqueror and decided that he would do better for himself if he helped depose the Conqueror and install Waltheof, an English earl, in his place as a puppet king. His principal partner in this enterprise was Ralf, Earl of Norfolk, but the pair found William too strong for them. The result was that the FitzOsbern family lost Chepstow and it became crown property for forty years. This diversion did not check the Norman penetration of Wales. An example of their strategic advance is shown by the four castles of Skenfrith, Grosmont, White- castle and Abergavenny. Abergavenny is the point of the arrow of penetration. South-east of Abergavenny is Monmouth, and from Monmouth the chain of castles extends in a south-westerly direction through Usk, Caerleon and Newport. North of Hereford, partly as a springboard for further invasion and partly as a counter to a sudden Welsh attack there was another series of castles: Wigmore, Ewyas Harold and Clifford. Wigmore was destined to play a significant part in history but, after the Middle Ages, fell into ruin and became overgrown. Recently attempts have been made to clear the site: even in its neglected state there are fewer more impressive castles. Clifford would be the home of 'Fair Rosamund', mistress of Henry II; she was eventually buried in Godstow Nunnery which caused the other nuns no little annoyance.

Some of the Marcher lords, the holders of castles on the border between England and Wales, soon became so entwined in Welsh politics through treaties or marriage, that they took the Welsh side in disputes. Glyndwr's son-in-law, Mortimer, starved to death in the siege of Harlech castle. Apart from the better known castles there are scores of small mottes – usually marked on the ordnance survey map – where the traveller can climb on the mound, assess the purpose and success of the builder and ponder why that one remained a motte and was never translated into a stone castle like so many of its fellows.

The danger from without had not the least effect on Welsh internal politics, as the Normans quickly appreciated. They thereupon looked for every opportunity to exploit the differences. Roger of Montgomery, Earl of Shrewsbury, made an alliance with Caradoc, one of the men who had fought with some success against the late King Harold. Together Roger and Caradoc fought the army of Meredith ap Owen, thereby opening up south Wales. Then in the north a rebellion flared up in which Bleddyn, King of Gwynedd, was killed. The throne of Wales was once more empty. Although Bleddyn's nephew Cynwric had succeeded it did not seem as if he would have the skill to retain the throne. And now a new contender appeared upon the scene, an outsider. This was Griffith ap Conan. This man was part Danish, part Irish, but also descended from the old royal line of Gwynedd. He had an army, mainly Irish, and he arrived with it at Deganwy. He demanded that the people of Gwynedd should depose Cynwric and accept him as their king. They said neither yes nor no. They had no special objection to Cynwric and for the moment their relations with their neighbours were peaceful.

It did not seem that peace would long be preserved if this wild-looking claimant took the throne. And the people of Gwynedd had had enough of internal dissent for the time being. There was more than enough to do in keeping out the Normans.

Griffith, impatiently, sailed on from Deganwy. He reached the Clwyd and there he came to the castle recently built by Robert of Rhuddlan; the motte is still there to be seen, close to the later Edwardian castle. Robert was famous for his oppression and cruelty but he was also cunning; he looked at the newcomer and thought he might offer him friendship and then use him. He therefore greeted him in a friendly manner and eventually lent him some soldiers. Griffith returned to Deganwy, picked up recruits from Anglesey and then met Cynwric in open battle at a site unknown. Cynwric was killed, Griffith then defeated Cynwric's cousin Trahaiam at a place named Bloody Acre but did not manage to kill him. Robert of Rhuddlan now hoped to share in the spoils but was told there were none for him. Not wishing to provoke a conflict in territory so unsuitable to his soldiers he returned to Rhuddlan, to bide his time.

Inevitably the combination of Griffith, and Irish and Welsh supporters from outside Gwynedd would lead to trouble. The first rebellion brought him to battle at Bron yr Erw and he was lucky to escape with his life. But escape he did. Soon he was back with a fleet which was augmented by pirates. Unfortunately for Griffith the latter required money rather than nebulous promises, and as Griffith could not produce it they withdrew their support. Griffith's attempt to restore himself had failed. This seemed to the Normans an appropriate time to consolidate their grasp on north Wales. A swift thrust took them all the way to Deganwy. But this made little difference to Griffith's plans. There would be time enough to deal with the Normans later, he hoped. Meanwhile he picked up an ally in Rees ap Tudor, an exile from south Wales who had recently been living in Brittany and with him challenged Trahaiam, King of Powys and cousin to the late Bleddyn, whom he had twice before fought. The ensuing battle fought in 1079 was called Mynydd Cam. Unlike most medieval battles it lasted through the day and far into the night. There seems to have been an interesting mixture of weapons on this day for the Irish were using long spears and their opponents mainly two-edged battleaxes. Griffith was victorious and now became undisputed King of Wales. However, the Normans were now poised to make a further thrust.

The Norman drive into Wales was now led by Bernard de Neufmarche, whose father had been a trusted supporter of William the Conqueror. Bernard requested permission to conquer territory for himself. Norman policy was to allot a piece of territory and then tell the aspirant to go and conquer it. In the first flush of victory after Hastings, most of Britain had been handed out in huge grants of land to those who had been with William in the critical battle. A few English who had not opposed him at Hastings were allowed to retain their land on his harsh terms. The result was that for the bellicose younger sons of Norman landowners there was nothing to share out unless fresh territories were conquered. Scotland offered some possibilities for new conquests but it was far away; Wales offered much better prospects, or so it seemed. The Welsh, as the Normans found, were not prepared to give up their territories lightly but periodically would engage in suicidal internal wars leaving the way open for the invader.

Bernard de Neufmarche began his career just before William the Conqueror died. He began by building a castle at Talgarth, and followed it by building one at Brecon. He may have built an early castle at Crickhowell. These moves gave him control of the area of Brycheiniog but he did not hold it easily. His new castle at Brecon was constantly under attack. These attacks and many more on Norman strongholds were undoubtedly the inspiration of Griffith but the Welsh king's career was now destined for another setback. Griffith was no great diplomat although apparently not without culture when he wished to show this side of his nature. In an attempt to obtain the co-operation of some of his more disaffected subjects he agreed to attend a meeting of tribal chiefs. But his reception had been prepared for him with nauseating treachery. He was ambushed near Corwen by a Norman force and taken off to prison at Chester. There was little now to stop the Normans except individual pockets of Welsh resistance. And these could not keep them out for long.

Hugh of Montgomery now came back to Dyfed which he had briefly visited twenty years before. He built Cilgerran castle, two miles south-east of Cardigan, on the left bank of the Teifi. It is doubtful whether this was actually on the exact site of the present castle for there are traces of several early castles in the area. Sometimes the only relic of a former castle is the name of a street or a place- Bailey Street, Castle Fields, Barbican Walk. The enthusiast will be able to take such clues and probably define the area of the castle. Similar clues exist on little-known battlefields but these are usually more macabre: Red Hill, Bloody Meadow, or Grave Hollow.

Norman names were now penetrating through south Wales and as they went were sometimes linked with those of the former holders of the lands. Richard of Granville built Neath Castle and Maurice of London built Kidwelly. The latter's father had established the strategically valuable castle at Ogmore. Kidwelly and Ogmore were both destined to play a distinguished part in Welsh history. There was already a castle at Coity, just over a mile north of Bridgend. It was owned by a man named Morgan. There is a remarkable story attached to Coity. The major Norman baron in south Wales at this time was Robert FitzHamon. From his base at Gloucester he launched attacks into south Wales, through Gwent into what was known as Morgannwy, which is now roughly the area of Glamorgan. He had established himself powerfully at Cardiff by building a motte inside the old Roman fortress. The visitor to Cardiff will see part of the old Roman wall, FitzHamon's motte, and later buildings, many of which are the results of the genius of the nineteenth-century architect, William Burges, financed by the enormously wealthy third Marquess of Bute. FitzHamon rewarded eleven of his faithful knights but overlooked the claims of Payn de Turbeville. Payn thereupon asked where his lands might be and was told that he could have men and equipment but he would have to find his own estate.

With this peculiar charter Payn presented himself at Coity castle and suggested to Morgan that he should hand over his castle without a struggle. Morgan, considering that the force accompanying Payn was formidable enough without the backing it would eventually receive, decided to be diplomatic. He brought out his daughter Sybil and said if Payn would marry her she should have the castle as her dowry. If he would not have her the ownership of the castle should be settled by a simple duel between Morgan and Payn. Such is the legend, which may well be true in its essentials. Payn chose to marry Sybil but soon was aligning himself with the Welsh princes against his own Norman allies. He was not the first, nor would he be the last, to support the fortunes of the Welsh however dubious the prospect seemed. Other castles of this period were Cowbridge and Llanbleddian. There were still parts of Wales which the Normans had not conquered, even in the less hilly areas. One was the district of Deheubarth, around Dynevor.

The statement 'the Normans conquered Wales', which sometimes appears in history books, gives a false impression. The Normans penetrated Wales, sometimes being engaged in skirmishes, sometimes being ambushed, and sometimes making alliances with one faction against another. But it is one thing to march along the roads and build castles at intervals; it is quite another to impose one's will on a conquered people. Wales presented special problems. The type of castle which was perfectly satisfactory in other countries was shown to have many deficiencies when used in Wales. Walls, whether of wood or stone, needed to be exceptionally high if they were to keep out the agile Welsh. Travel, too, was never safe in Wales. A party of Normans crossing a ford might be surprised and indignant at being ambushed in what was now thought to be settled and friendly territory. The ambush party, however, might well not come from the locality at all but be a raiding party from some distance away. It was fatal, often literally fatal, to assume you could travel in safety in Wales. Giraldus Cambrensis quotes the example of Richard de Clare, who, in approximately 1140, was journeying in Wales. He says:

'This nobleman of high birth and lord of Cardiganshire passed this way [near Abergavenny], accompanied by Brian de Wallingford, lord of this province and many men-at-arms. At the passage of Coed Grono and at the entrance to the wood, he dismissed him and his attendants, though much against their will, and proceeded on his journey un-armed; from too great a presumption of security preceded only by a minstrel and a singer, one accompanying the other on a fiddle. The Welsh awaiting his arrival, with Iorweth, brother of Morgan of Carleon at their head, and others of his family, rushed upon him unawares from the thickets and killed him and many of his followers.'

It seems that Morgan had a long-standing grievance against the de Clare family and had long awaited such an opportunity. The de Clare family seemed to prosper in spite of miscalculations such as this and also in spite of occasionally supporting the losing side in a rebellion against the reigning monarch. The occasion indicates another side of Welsh history and attitudes. Real or imagined wrongs, and usually they were real enough, were not forgotten. Instead the Welsh pondered on them and meditated revenge. Opportunity might be long in coming, perhaps a family might have to wait a generation. However, in time the chance would come and vengeance would be exacted in full measure. In most cases the revenge would lead to reprisals later. A long memory is not always a blessing.

We left Griffith ap Conan in prison in Chester. In those days it was the custom to load prisoners with chains but often to allow them freedom to move around as much as their fetters allowed. On one occasion when most of the castle guard was drunk, a Welshman walked in, lifted up Griffith and carried him out to safety. Griffith's subsequent career was nothing if not spectacular. Initially he waged guerrilla warfare from the mountains of Snowdonia, then slipped over to Ireland, collected a fleet and recaptured Anglesey from the Normans. With a secure base he was now able to carry the war to the enemy. In a raid on Deganwy he killed his treacherous former ally, Robert of Rhuddlan. Soon the rest of north and west Wales was up in arms too. The king on the English throne at this time was William Rufus (1087–1100). Rufus was not the Conqueror's eldest son but he was the man on the spot when the Conqueror's death was known in England. Rufus's court was the essence of depravity but when it came to fighting there were few to equal 'the Red King'. Even Bernard de Neufmarchd rebelled against Rufus and mustered a combined English/ Welsh army. The ensuing war ebbed and flowed. Rufus left his Marcher barons to restore the situation in Wales. The Welsh harried and massacred the Normans where and when they could: the Normans blinded, mutilated, castrated or executed any Welsh they could lay their hands on. At the end of three years the situation had settled, mainly through the exhaustion of both sides. The only stable part of Wales was around Pembroke where Gerald of Windsor held the castle against all comers. There were Flemings now living in Pembroke to add to the amalgam of races in Wales.

On this stage now appears one of the most remarkable women of history. This was the Princess Nest or Nesta. She was the daughter of Rees ap Tudor, the last King of Deheubarth, and was apparently astonishingly beautiful. She was also what would nowadays be called 'highly sexed'. While little more than a girl she was taken to London as a hostage for her father and resided at Henry I's court. Henry was a severe king but he enjoyed his pleasures and he did not fail to take advantage of the Welsh princess's presence. She bore him a son – Henry Fitzhenry. She was then returned to Wales where she was married to Gerald of Windsor, Henry I's castle-holder at Pembroke. She bore him five children but was abducted one night by her cousin, Owen of Cadogan (Owain ap Cadwgan). This led to a bitter feud. Gerald had been lucky to escape with his life in the attack during which Nesta had been abducted. Owen of Cadogan's father was horrified at his son's stupid and thoughtless act and tried to persuade him to hand back Nesta. Owen refused but had to flee to Ireland and lost the family lands. Eventually old Cadogan bought his old lands back on the strict condition that Owen must not be allowed to return. However, the father was quite unable to restrain a son as wild as Owen and the result was that Owen ravaged the countryside while the father once more lost his lands. Owen, however, was not destined to last much longer. He met Gerald of Windsor by chance on a lonely road and the latter was able to exact revenge by killing his wife's abductor. Gerald died soon after and Nesta now married Stephen, the Constable of Cardigan. To him she bore even more sons. Nesta's three families all took part in the conquest of Ireland and were the founders of famous Irish dynasties, the Fitzhenries, Fitzgeralds and Fitzstephens. The Welsh branch of the Fitzgeralds adopted the name Carew.

Visitors to Dyfed should not miss visiting Carew Castle, four miles east of Pembroke. No part of this interesting castle dates back to the days when it was Nesta's dowry to Gerald of Windsor, but it is still rich in history and legend. In 1485, when Henry Tudor, later Henry VII of England, was marching to meet Richard III at Bosworth Field he stayed overnight at Carew. The castle was besieged in the Civil War in 1642 but did not resist for long. But there are macabre stories about the ghosts at Carew Castle. During the sixteenth century it was lost to the Carews for a time and granted to Sir John Perrot. Perrot was said to be an illegitimate son of Henry VIII but this did not prevent him being accused of plotting against Queen Elizabeth I and dying in the Tower of London in 1592. Apparently he was a staunch Catholic and there are said to be secret passages under the castle which the priests used. His ghost is said to haunt the Great Hall, which he built and which is still very beautiful even in ruins. But an even more impressive ghost is that of Sir Roland Rhys. His son married the daughter of a Flemish tradesman named Horwitz, who was one of his tenants. One night when the girl's father had come to the castle to pay his rent he had been unable to return owing to a storm. Sir Roland had a pet ape which in a moment of anger he had set to attack Horwitz, but in the middle of the night there was an extraordinary scene in which apparently the ape killed its master and pulled the fire out of the hearth. The ape was burnt to death and the hall partly destroyed. Needless to say all these scenes form part of the hauntings – or so the story goes.

Giraldus Cambrensis was the grandson of Nesta through her daughter Angharad who had married William de Barri. Barri was a Norman nobleman but Giraldus never thought of himself as anything but a Welshman. He was brought up in Manorbier castle which he describes with loving care. Manorbier is beautifully preserved and today's visitor is able to gain some impression of what it once must have looked like. It contains a lifelike representation of Giraldus writing in his room. As a young man he studied in Paris and visited Rome. He was court chaplain to Henry II and often travelled around France with that restless monarch. Although he retired to Lincoln he never lost his deep love for Manorbier.

But affection for Wales did not blind Giraldus to the weaknesses of the Welsh. Among these weaknesses was a credulity which he exploited to good account. Possibly be-cause he was not satisfied that churches were treated sufficiently reverently he quoted the case of the lord of Builth castle. One night he 'entered the church of Llan Avan and without sufficient caution or reverence, had passed the night there with his hounds. Arising early in the morning, according to the custom of hunters, he found his hounds mad and himself struck blind.' That was a sobering story for anyone thinking of sheltering with his dogs overnight in a church.

Some of his examples were drawn from outside Wales. In Hovedene 'the concubine of the rector incautiously sat down on the tomb of St Osana, which projected like a wooden seat; on wishing to retire she could not be removed until people came to her assistance; her clothes were rent, her body laid bare and severely afflicted with many strokes of discipline, even till the blood flowed ...' No mention is made of the rector during these occurrences!

At the vigil of St Kenelm in Gloucestershire large numbers of women flocked to the monastery, and 'the under butler of that convent committed fornication within the precincts of the monastery. This same man on the following day had the audacity to carry the psalter in the procession of saints; and on his return to the choir, after the solemnity the psalter stuck to his hands.' A full confession and considerable penitence eventually led to his being freed from this embarrassing situation ... Giraldus gives us an insight into some of the customs of the time with considerable realism. At Haverford, Dyfed:

A famous robber was fettered and confined in one of the towers and was often visited by three boys, the son of the Earl of Clare and two others, one of whom was son of the lord of the castle and the other his grandson, who applied to him for arrows with which he used to supply them. One day, at the request of the children the robber, being brought from his dungeon, took advantage of the absence of the gaoler, closed the door and shut himself up with the boys . . . nor did he cease with uplifted axe to threaten the lives of the children until indemnity and security were assured to him in the most ample manner.

A similar accident happened at Chateau Roux in France. The lord of that place maintained in the castle a man whose eyes had formerly been put out but who, by long habit, recollected the ways of the castle and the steps leading to the towers. Seizing an opportunity of revenge and meditating destruction of the youth he fastened the inward doors of the castle and took the only son and heir of the governor to the summit of a high tower from whence he was seen with the utmost concern by the people beneath. The father of the boy hastened thither and, struck with terror, attempted by every possible means to secure the ransom of his son, but received for answer that this could not be effected but by the mutilation of those lower parts by which he had likewise inflicted on him. The father, having in vain entreated mercy, at length assented and caused a violent blow to be struck at his body, and the people cried out lamentably, as if he had suffered mutilation. The blind man asked him where he felt the greatest pain and when he replied in his reins he declared it was false and prepared to precipitate the boy. A second blow was given and the lord of the castle asserting that the greatest pains were at his heart, the blind man expressing disbelief again carried the boy to the summit of the tower. The third time, however, the father, to save his son really mutilated himself and when he explained that the greatest pain was his teeth [received the reply] 'It is true, as a man who has had experience should be believed and thou hast in part revenged my injuries. I shall meet death with more satisfaction and thou shalt neither beget any other son nor receive comfort from this.' Then precipitating himself and the boy from the summit of the tower their limbs were broken and both instantly expired.

Doubtless Giraldus heard this horrific story during his travels in France. The custom of keeping former enemies in fetters and on view in fortresses dates back to many centuries before Giraldus's time. The object of the exercise is not clear unless it was to provide an odd job man who could use his hands for mending bows, sharpening weapons, making arrows, or merely amusing children. There are other recorded examples when the manacled prisoner seized an important passer-by as a hostage and obtained his revenge. There was little point in his negotiating for his release, for as soon as the bargain had been made and the hostage released the prisoner would have been killed.

Pembroke, which he calls Penbroch, is given as the scene of a siege in the reign of Henry I (1100–35). He describes it at the time as 'a slender fortress with stables and turf so it is clearly a tall narrow motte (motte was Norman-French for turf) with palisades on top and at the base. This he consigned to the care of Giraldus de Windsor, his con-stable and lieutenant-general, a worthy and discreet man. Immediately on the death of Rhys son of Tewdr who a short time before had been slain by the treachery of his own troops at Brecheinoc, leaving his son Gruffyd a child, the inhabitants of south

Wales besieged the castle. One night when fifteen soldiers had deserted, and endeavoured to escape from the castle in a small boat, on the following morning Giraldus invested their armour-bearers with the arms and estates of their masters and decorated them with the military order. The garrison being, from the length of the seige, reduced to the utmost want of provisions, the constable, with great providence and flattering hopes of success, caused four hogs, which yet remained, to be cut into small pieces and thrown down to the enemy from the fortifications. The next day, having again recourse to more refined stratagem, he contrived that a letter, sealed with his own signet, should be found before the house of Wilfred, Bishop of St David's, who was then by chance in that neighbourhood, as if accidentally dropped, stating that there would be no necessity of soliciting the assistance of the earl Amulph for the next four months to come. The contents of these letters being made known to the army, the troops abandoned the siege of the castle and retired to their own homes.

Psychological warfare of this type was widely practised in the Middle Ages. Agents were sometimes sent to places where they would be captured whereupon the false information they were carrying would be believed. The pieces of hog were meant to show that there was so much food in the castle that large pieces could be tossed contemptuously to the enemy. As surrender through starvation was the fate of many a castle in the Middle Ages, any strategy which could persuade the besiegers that protracting the siege was hopeless was of great value. Approximately the same story is told of Carcassonne in southern France. There a pig was allowed to 'escape' and fall from the battlements. When it hit the ground it burst open, showing its stomach to be full of grain. This was meant to persuade the besiegers that the castle held so much grain that it could even be fed to pigs.

Deception of every type was frequent. On the battlements at Chepstow are dummy figures representing archers. These were meant to confuse the attacker and delude him into thinking that the castle was more heavily garrisoned than in fact it was. Similar deception targets appear on the battlements at Alnwick, Northumberland. Although most of the figures are of later manufacture they replace earlier genuine ones.

Although the Welsh were adept at guile and deception their ability in these were not their only military arts. Already in the twelfth century they were skilled in the use of the longbow. Bows and arrows had been known from prehistoric times, and in the twelfth century one of the most feared weapons was the crossbow, on account of its range and power. The crossbow was the only weapon by which an inferior could seriously threaten the armoured knight. Usually on the battlefield, protected by armour and mounted, the knight was immune to all but a lucky pike thrust or an attack by another knight. However, a crossbow was an elaborate weapon even in its simplest form, and its effectiveness depended greatly on the complexity of its winding gear. It had the advantage that it could be used by a weak man or even a youngster but it was slow in operation and seldom discharged more than two bolts (arrows) a minute.

From south Wales came a new weapon, the longbow, destined in its time to be as terrifying as modern weapons of mass murder. A true longbow was some six feet long and discharged an arrow of approximately three feet. Arrows were of various types, some with narrow points for piercing between the links of armour and some with broader heads for slicing through the rigging on ships. They had an effective range of some 240 yards but when flighted could cover twice that distance. A favourite expedient was to launch a stream of arrows high into the air, so that in falling they would descend almost vertically on a body of horsemen. The horses, maddened by the pain of their wounds, would rear and throw their riders who would be stunned and perhaps trampled on in the fall. At this scene of dismay and confusion would suddenly appear the Welsh 'dagger-men' who would quickly finish off anyone unlikely to be worth a ransom and more often than not someone who was. The tendency of the 'dagger-men' to rush in and dispose of the fallen made them extremely unpopular, not only with their opponents, who might otherwise hope to recover from a small wound, but also with their own fellows who would heartily curse the habit of slaughtering valuable hostages, or ransom- able prisoners. But it proved exceedingly difficult to control Welsh soldiers once their battle fury was roused. Most archers carried hammers which were designed for driving in wooden stakes in front of defended positions (chevaux de frise) but they were often misused to crack the armour of a fallen knight and let in the murderous dagger. The full power of the Welsh archers would not be seen till Crecy, Poitiers and Agincourt, but their ability was noteworthy in the twelfth century. Giraldus states that in one of the endless fights around Abergavenny castle the following incident took place.

In the last capture of the aforesaid castle, which happened in our days, two soldiers passing over the bridge to take refuge in a tower built on a mound of earth, the Welsh taking them in the rear, penetrated with their arrows the oaken portal of the tower, which was four fingers thick, in memory of which circumstance the arrows were preserved in the gate.

Nearly four inches of penetration into solid oak seems almost incredible but the performance was not unique. Giraldus went on:

'William de Braose also testifies that one of his soldiers in a conflict with the Welsh was wounded by an arrow which passed through his thigh and the armour with which it was cased on both sides and through that part of the saddle, which is called the alva, mortally wounded the horse. Another soldier had his hip, equally sheafed in armour, penetrated by an arrow quite to the saddle and on turning the horse round received a similar wound on the opposite hip, which fixed him on both sides of his seat. Yet the bows used by this people are not made of horn, ivory or yew but of wild elm, unpolished, rude and uncouth but stout, not calculated to shoot an arrow to a great distance but to inflict very severe wounds in close fight.'

There was, however, more than one disadvantage to the longbow. It had a 60–70 lb. pull which meant that the archer must be a strong and well-trained man. It was not usually required to be accurate, for its rapid rate of discharge, averaging twelve arrows a minute, could blanket a target on which they descended like a dark vengeful cloud. The recipients would suddenly notice that the sky had gone dark and there was a curious sound like the hissing of geese. In the next moment all would be groans, screams and confusion. Those who live in more civilized times will probably recollect experiences in the Second World War when the sound of bombs falling through the air resembled that of coal being poured into a cellar. It is a sound only heard before the first bomb arrives and explodes. Sounds of falling missiles, whether arrows or bombs, tend to be intimidating because there is no means of judging whether they are going to land close by or far away. A shell or bullet which you can hear will probably miss you; not so an arrow or bomb.

Some of Giraldus's stories of the activities of the men of south Wales recall the troubles the Romans had from the Silurians. One of the most extraordinary stories of daring kidnap concerns Cardiff castle. He describes the castle as being surrounded by high walls, which could be the old Roman walls and thus a considerable deterrent, and containing a hundred and twenty men-at-arms and a numerous body of archers. The town itself, which adjoined the castle, was full of Norman soldiers. There was also a supposedly efficient system of sentries. Nearby was a man named Ivor the Little, 'a man of short stature but great courage'. Ivor owned a tract of mountainous and woody country, of which the holder of the castle, William, Earl of Gloucester, had recently, quite unjustly, deprived him; the Normans were noted for their acquisitiveness even when its gratification did more harm than good. A visitor to Cardiff castle today would consider that the Earl of Gloucester, safely housed in the keep on the mound, inside the Roman walls, and at every point surrounded by his soldiers would have been safe enough.

Yet in defiance of all these precautions of security, Ivor, in the dead of night, secretly scaled the walls, and seizing the Earl and Countess, with their only son, carried them off into the woods and did not release them until he had recovered everything that had been unjustly taken from him and received compensation of additional property.

The feat might seem impossible, but it was accomplished. To have crept into the castle and killed the earl or to have taken the child as a hostage, though extremely difficult, seems practicable. But to remove the earl, his wife, and son back through the ring of defenders almost defies imagination. Doubtless some had been bribed or even made drunk but it would not have been possible to subvert an entire garrison. Well might Ivor be a popular name in Wales.

The castle walls at Abergavenny, previously thought to be unscaleable, were climbed in 1182. The event is glossed over by Giraldus for it concerns the patron of his living. This was William de Braose. The Braose family held Bramber castle in Sussex but most of their nefarious activities were concluded in south Wales. Near Abergavenny was a small Welsh lordship of which the holder was Sitsyllt ap Dyfnwal. Their manor was at Penpergwm and had the name of Casde Arnold. Sitsyllt was no model of restrained and decorous behaviour; he was as turbulent as most of his contemporaries and he had killed William de Braose's uncle in a fight some time before. De Braose was his feudal overlord and summoned Sitsyllt and other local lords to Abergavenny for a feast and the hearing of a royal proclamation. As soon as they were seated de Braose's soldiers massacred the lot. This was followed by an even worse atrocity in which a party went to the now undefended Castle Arnold and murdered Sitsyllt's son. This was in 1175.

Sitsyllt's kin spent the next eight years planning revenge. In 1182 a large party crept up to the castle and scaled the unscaleable walls. Unfortunately, de Braose was not there and their revenge was mainly executed on his soldiers. It was some years before nemesis overtook William de Braose, who eventually died in exile. By that time he had fallen foul of King John (though not over the Magna Carta) and fled to France. John, enraged at having missed de Braose, contented himself with imprisoning his wife and son and starving them to death. John was addicted to this unpleasant method of putting to death those who had incurred his displeasure.

The portrait of the twelfth-century Welsh character painted by Giraldus is not usually flattering but is certainly interesting. He describes his countrymen as light and active, hardy rather than strong and entirely bred up to the use of arms; for not only the nobles but all the people are trained to war, and when the trumpet sounds the alarm the husbandman rushes as eagerly from his plough as the courtier from his court . . . they anxiously study the defence of their country and their liberty; for these they fight, for these they undergo hardships; and for these willingly sacrifice their lives; they esteem it a disgrace to die in bed, an honour to die in the field of battle. They make use of light arms which do not impede their agility, small coats of mail, bundles of arrows and long lances, helmets and shields, and more rarely greaves [leg shields] plated with iron. The higher class go to battle mounted on swift and generous steeds, which their country produces, but the greater part of the people fight on foot on account of the marshy nature and unevenness of the soil. The horsemen, as their situation or occasion requires, willingly serve as infantry, in attacking or retreating and they either walk barefooted, or make use of high shoes, roughly constructed with untanned leather. In time of peace the young men, by penetrating the deep recesses of the woods and climbing the tops of mountains, learn by practice to endure fatigue through day and night; and as they meditate on war during peace they acquire the art of fighting by accustoming themselves to the use of the lance and by inuring themselves to hard exercise.

Henry II described the Welsh, in reply to an enquiry from a foreign monarch, as 'so bold and ferocious that when un-armed they did not fear to encounter an armed force; being ready to shed their blood in defence of their country, and to sacrifice their lives for renown.'

Giraldus speaks highly of Welsh frugality, hospitality and liberality, their interest in music, general culture, wit and articulate speech. However he notes that their love of high birth and ancient genealogy makes them all too prone to 'revenge with vehemence the injuries which may tend to disgrace their blood and being naturally of vindictive and passionate disposition they are ever ready to avenge not only recent but ancient affronts'.

However their faults also extend to a long catalogue. He describes them as 'no less light in mind than in body' and says, 'they never scruple at taking a false oath for the sake of any temporary emolument or advantage'. Harsh though this criticism is it appears to be borne out by the senseless internal wars and feuds which characterized the period.

He also goes into some detail on the manner in which the Welsh conduct themselves on the battlefield. He is critical of them but in fact the technique is that of guerrilla forces everywhere. In war this nation is very severe in the first attack, terrible by their clamour and looks, filling the air with horrid shouts and the deep-toned clangour of very long trumpets, swift and rapid in their advances and frequent throwing of darts. Bold in the first onset, they cannot bear a repulse, being easily thrown into confusion as soon as they turn their backs, and they trust to flight for safety, without attempting to rally. The character given to the Teutons in the Roman history may be applied to this people. In their first attack they are more than men, in the second less than women. Their courage manifests itself chiefly in the retreat, when they return and, like the Parthians, shoot their arrows behind them, and as after success and victory in battle even cowards boast of their courage so after a reverse of fortune even the bravest men are not allowed their due claims of merit. Their mode of fighting consists in chasing the enemy or retreating. This light-armed people, relying more on their activity than their strength, cannot struggle for the field of battle, enter into close engagement, or endure long and severe actions.

Nevertheless he goes on to pay them a great compliment.

Though defeated and put to flight on one day they are ready to resume the combat on the next, neither dejected by their loss nor by their dishonour and although perhaps they do not display great fortitude in open engagements and regular conflicts, yet they harass the enemy by ambuscades and nightly sallies. Hence neither oppressed by hunger or cold, nor fatigued by martial labours, nor despondent in adversity, but ready after defeat to return immediately to action and again endure the dangers of war they are as easy to overcome in a single battle as difficult to subdue in a protracted war.

There seems to be an extraordinary complexity of activities in ordinary Welsh life. He mentions that the people are particularly addicted to digging up boundary limits, and land-marks. They also produce a variety of property claims which keep the jurors busy. The custom of distributing land equally among brothers seems to have led to suits and contentions, murders and conflagrations, and frequent fratricides. Another hearty grievance also prevails; the princes entrust the education of their children to the care of the principal men of their country, each of whom, after the death of his father, endeavours by every possible means to exalt his own charge above his neighbour. It is also remarkable that brothers show more affection to each other when dead than when living for they persecute the living even unto death but revenge the deceased with all their power.

In spite of the frugality and civilized behaviour which he praised earlier, Giraldus produces an entirely contrary account in his general description. Now he says they are 'immoderate in their love of food and intoxicating drink . . . When seated at another man's table after long fasting their appetite is immoderate.' He also states that incest is wide-spread at all levels of society, but by this he probably meant intermarriage with close relations. 'They do not engage in marriage until they have tried by previous cohabitation the disposition and particularly the fecundity of the person with whom they are engaged.' This, of course, was normal practice in many nations for no man wished to be married to an infertile wife.

Although Giraldus tends to be critical of his fellow countrymen, it seems unlikely that they were worse than most European peoples living at the time and were probably a good deal better than most. It is clear that they had tremendous vitality, enterprise, and resilience. Their resourcefulness is shown by the fact that when confronted by an armoured knight they developed the best weapon to combat him, just as badly-equipped people, when faced with tanks, devise crude petrol bombs to harass them. The longbow was originally the weapon of south Wales but in time it spread to the north too. Before the advent of the longbow the men of north Wales made effective use of lances which they threw with deadly accuracy and force. Although both these weapons have long been obsolete it would be a mistake to underrate their killing power when used in quantity and under the right conditions.

History owes a great deal to Giraldus. Not only does he give us a wealth of details we would otherwise not know but he sets them down in a fluent and readable way. Even when he is distressed at some happening or habit, he never becomes petulant or tedious. The Welsh may well be proud of such a skilled chronicler.

Chapter 5

THE BATTLES OF OWEN GWYNEDD

Griffith ap Conan died in 1137 after a career of astonishing vicissitudes. His daughter Gwenllian married Griffith ap Rees, ruler of Deheubarth. After the death of Henry I of England in 1135 there was a complete absence of control or direction from London as the country was torn between the rival claims of Stephen and Matilda. All over England barons were using the state of anarchy to feather their nests and plunder their neighbours. The Norman castle-holders in Wales were by no means averse to unrestricted licence but they found that the anarchy which deprived them of reinforcements was no advantage. Indeed they were more vulnerable to Welsh attack. Griffith ap Rees decided that the time was ripe to oust the Normans from Deheubarth. Somewhat to his surprise the Normans in Wales made common cause and marched against him. Griffith ap Rees, hearing the news, went to get help from his wife's father but his absence was longer than anticipated and the Normans were soon marching into his territory. They were confronted at Kidwelly by an army led by Gwenllian, a veritable Joan of Arc, but she was defeated and lost her life in the process. But up in the north the armies were rallying. The armies met on the northern side of the Teifi at Cardigan in 1136. This was no skirmish between a few barefooted spearmen and a detachment of lumbering ironclads but a full scale battle in which the Welsh are said to have numbered eight thousand of which two thousand were armoured horsemen. The details of the battle are lost but it seems most probable that it would have begun with a shower of arrows and spears from the Welsh foot and continued with a charge by the Welsh horse. The upshot of it was that the Norman force was sent staggering back and as they tried to retire over the bridge had the additional misfortune of hearing it crack under them. Many were drowned and perhaps they were the lucky ones. The Welsh drove on to recapture the Norman castle and re-distribute the lands of which they felt they had been robbed.

This battle at Cardigan is little known although it was a major event. However the earlier encounter, in which Gwenllian was killed, stayed in men's minds for centuries. Gwenllian had been born in Anglesey in 1097 and was strikingly beautiful, but by the time she met Griffith ap Rees old Griffith ap Conan had had enough of wars and was prepared to settle for peace with the Normans. Gwenllian eloped and for a long time she and her husband lived in the woods fighting the Normans as guerrillas. There are conflicting stories of what happened at Kidwelly. Some say that her 'army' became restless at her husband's long absence and to give them something to do she decided to attack Kidwelly Castle, then held by the detested Maurice de Londres. She was captured alive, begged for mercy but was beheaded by Maurice's order. The land close to Kidwelly is known as 'the field of the grave of Gwenllian' (Maes Gwenllian). The fact that Kidwelly Castle is in ruins is said to be the curse upon it. For centuries Welshmen would go to war crying 'Revenge for Gwenllian' without any idea of who Gwenllian might have been. Although martyred by the circumstances of her death, Gwenllian was scarcely a fighter for freedom. While living in the woods with her husband she caused endless trouble by bringing reprisals on to the innocent, as 'Robin Hoods' often do.

In his closing years, Griffith ap Conan had hoped that his two sons Cadwaladr and Owen Gwynedd would work in harmony to ensure the future of the kingdom he had so carefully built up in spite of so many setbacks. However their characters contrasted strongly, Cadwaladr being brave, headstrong and completely bored by peace, and Owen much more statesmanlike and cautious though also a talented soldier. At first all went well. Owen stayed in Gwynedd making it stronger and more prosperous; Cadwaladr went to the west coast where there was always fighting to be done. The union of all Wales seemed well on the way to fulfilment when Anarawd, son of Griffith ap Rees was to marry one of Owen's daughters. The inability of the Normans to win back their lost territory and the chaos in England caused by the Stephen-Matilda anarchy meant that the Welsh were left to work out their own destiny. And for a time all seemed harmonious beyond all reasonable expectation.

Hope was shattered in 1143, on the very eve of Anarawd's marriage to Owen's daughter, for at that moment Cadwaladr killed Anarawd in a quarrel over a boundary dispute. It was the sort of dispute which had happened many times before in Welsh history but never had it had such wide-reaching effects as at that time.

Owen was in a desperate position. Should he support his brother against the rage of die southern princes or should he put the unity of Wales first? He made up his mind; Wales must live. He sent a force to Aberystwyth to burn Cadwaladr's castle and seize his lands. Cadwaladr became an exile. But there were precedents for Cadwaladr to follow and he followed them faithfully. His love for his brother turned to a bitter hatred which would stop at nothing. Cadwaladr made overtures to the Normans, who even in the anarchy could see the advantages of a divided Wales. From one end of Wales to the other the Norman barons went on to the attack. This was war on a national scale. In the south there was intermittent fighting but a general stalemate. Cadwaladr had returned to Cardigan and built himself a castle at Llan Rhystyd. Owen's main preoccupation was the castle at Mold, for while the Normans held that an attack on north Wales could be launched at any time. Owen besieged Mold but it long defied his efforts to reduce it; then in 1146 it fell. Unfortunately Mold today shows little sign of these events. The castle (which was originally built by Robert de Monte Alto and was then called Monte, not Mold) was demolished in the thirteenth century. All that remains today is the name 'Bailey Hill', which is a recreation ground.

With Mold castle in his hands Owen took fresh heart. Further south Meredith of Powys pushed east into Shropshire and built a castle at Oswestry. Cadwaladr was driven out of Cardigan and Wales was virtually united. At this moment the anarchy in England came to an end and the young resolute Angevin, Henry II, succeeded to the throne.

Henry had plenty to do. He did not take up his English throne for six weeks but instead occupied himself with tidying up the ever restless Anjou. Then he began demolishing the castles which had been built without royal licence during the anarchy. Finally he gave his attention to Wales. He was not so much concerned with the Welsh themselves but he knew very well that the Marcher lords would not hesitate to make alliance with Owen Gwynedd if they felt that would further their independence.

Henry's campaign followed traditional lines. A fleet went around the coast to Anglesey and the army set off from Chester heading for Rhuddlan. The main body marched along the coast, and Owen with his army grouped around Basingwerk was ready to receive them. Henry, hearing of the Welsh dispositions through spies, took off a detachment to catch Owen in the rear. To his surprise, he was himself intercepted by a detachment from Owen's army and nearly lost his life (at Coleshill?). Somewhat surprisingly Owen chose not to give battle but retreated slowly harassing the English army which then reached Rhuddlan. As Henry fortified the castle he pondered on the next move. The initiative seemed to have been taken from his hands. Then news reached him of disaster in Anglesey. Henry's fleet had gone ashore but had been attacked by the local people. Casualties had been high and among them was Henry Fitz-Henry, bastard son of Henry I and Nesta of Deheubarth. With astute diplomacy Owen decided this would be a good time to make peace with Henry.

Although victorious at that moment he knew that this situation could not last and neither he nor Henry wished for a long disruptive and expensive war. Henry backed Owen's plans for Welsh unity and in return was confirmed in his holding of strategic strongpoints in the north.

However, Henry could not always control his barons any more than Owen could prevent his own princelings quarrelling. There was trouble in the south, sometimes from lawless Norman barons, sometimes from jealous Welsh lords. Rees ap Griffith in Cardigan took the law into his own hands when Walter Clifford of Llandovery Castle started ravaging his lands. Soon an intermittent anarchic battle was disturbing the peace of west Wales. The solution to this, reasoned Owen, was to give Welsh arms employment outside Wales. He strengthened his position along the English border and came close to Chester. Henry understood Owen's predicament but couldn't approve his manner of settling it. In 1169 he was back with an army, determined to check Owen before Welsh armies began ravaging Hereford and Shropshire. This time, as he well knew, in spite of the dissensions of west Wales, the army Owen would bring against him was vastly more formidable than the one he had encountered twelve years before. The army Henry assembled for his task consisted mainly of mercenaries, hardened adventurers from Anjou, Normandy, Gascony and Flanders. They would neither give nor expect quarter. This time instead of coming up by Chester and Flint Henry decided to make a thrust past Oswestry along the Ceiriog and over the Berwyn hills. Owen quickly grasped Henry's intent and encamped his own army at Corwen. With luck and dry weather, Henry calculated that he could split Wales in half and send Owen's supporters scampering back to protect their own land within a month.

In the event matters proceeded differently. The Ceiriog valley proved unexpectedly difficult to negotiate, for it was heavily wooded and no commander with experience will ever try to take a large force through woods unless an adequate route has been cleared in advance. Clearing that path slowed the army down, supply was another major problem and the Welsh constantly harassed the mixed force. As Henry's soldiers struggled out of the valley they were lashed by storms of a ferocity they had never before experienced. There was clearly no hope of bringing Owen to battle here; there was in fact no alternative to humiliating retreat. Retreat they did, though they tried again in the north; and when they had withdrawn from the north too Owen was able to retake the castles at Prestatyn, Basingwerk and Rhuddlan, although the latter siege occupied three months. At the end of that year Owen died. He had reigned for thirty-two years, twice defeated Henry II and given Wales an example of how unity might be achieved. The formula was skill in battle and diplomacy and patience at all other times.

Although this book is mainly concerned with the military history of Wales, it should be mentioned that barons and lords, when not fighting, scheming or debauching themselves, often paid considerable deference to religion. Some went on Crusades, some endowed churches, and others founded monasteries and priories. Some, after a life of fighting and dubious practices, became monks themselves. One religious patron was Robert of Gloucester, yet another of Henry I's illegitimate sons. Robert supported his half-sister Matilda against Stephen in the years of anarchy (1135–52) but also even in those turbulent times, managed to establish the abbey of Margam. Margam was destined to become one of the most famous abbeys in Wales.

Chapter 6

THE BATTLES OF LLYWELYN AP IORWETH (LLYWELYN FAWR)

After the death of Owen Gwynedd the centre of Welsh unity shifted to Cardigan where, as we saw earlier, Rees ap Griffith was fighting off encroachments from the south and resisting turbulent Norman barons as well. He had rebuilt the castle at Cardigan and was clearly a man to be reckoned with. Henry II was now more concerned with what was going on in Ireland than in Wales and was glad to make a treaty with Rees whom he regarded as the right man to keep Wales stable at this time. In spite of having dealt firmly with baronial upstarts when he arrived on the throne, Henry II in 1174 had to face a baronial revolt. It was quickly quelled but he was glad to call on the assistance of Rees to help him suppress it. These were good years for Wales, and Rees, usually referred to as the Lord Rees, is something of a national hero. He was a great warrior and spent much of his time fortifying or fighting. Rhayader castle was greatly strengthened by him. In his later years he found himself in conflict with the English again, for after Henry II's death in 1189 the throne went to Richard I. Richard I, the Lionheart, was so lacking in interest in his English throne that he spent only eight months of his ten-year reign in England. In his absence his brother John ruled the country with casual inefficiency. John succeeded to the English throne on Richard's death in 1199 and held it till 1216. Llywelyn ap Iorweth obtained the throne of Gwynedd in 1194, half way through Richard's reign, held it all through John's reign and lived till 1240 which took him well into the reign of Henry III. Richard, as mentioned above, was mainly an absentee, John a very devious character though militarily capable. Henry III was under one year old at his succession and later very much under the influence of foreign favourites. Owen Gwynedd had left seven sons and had been succeeded by David (Daffyd). Another of Owen's sons was Madoc who many believe to have discovered America some three hundred years before Columbus set foot on that continent. Another son was Iorweth, who held Dolwyddelan castle, and it was at this castle that Llywelyn was born in 1173. Iorweth was apparently older than David but in the power struggle which had gone on after Owen's death David had emerged the victor. In 1194, when David was ruling over a divided and unhappy Gwynedd, Llywelyn considered the time right to claim what he considered to be his rightful inheritance. He raised a small army and defeated his uncle David at the battle of Aberconwy in 1194. David went into exile in Shropshire where he could hear of the problems of his supplanter. Llywelyn had spent most of his youth in England and learned to understand and negotiate with the English. He was able, forceful and ambitious. Sometimes he made mistakes, but usually he was able to extricate himself from the consequences.

His first six years were spent trying to consolidate his position. Apart from David waiting close at hand for a chance to regain lost power, there were other rivals in the remainder of Wales. Llywelyn's master stroke was to marry the daughter of King John, thereby making that monarch an ally and not an enemy. His first dangerous rival was Gwenwynwyn of Powys; in a combined operation he invaded and overran Powys while John captured his rival at Shrewsbury. With this good start he extended his power south and south-west, then captured the castles held by the Earl of Chester. These were those familiar, vital strongholds Deganwy, Rhuddlan, Mold and Holywell. This was an excellent record for only four years' consolidation, but the last move had been unwise. John, although not displeased to see a powerful baron like the Earl of Chester humiliated, was nevertheless not prepared to see Llywelyn, son-in-law or not, achieve this much power.

Once more, but not by any means for the last time, north Wales saw an invading army. This time it was made up of English from John's own resources and a host of discontented Welsh princes: Gwenwynwyn of Powys, Rees the Hoarse and Maelgwn. It was a formidable army and John, whatever his other faults, had nothing to learn about handling troops in battle. But as they tramped the road from Chester to Deganwy it was a barren land which met them. Llywelyn, realizing he could not hope to defeat this great army in open battle, fell back and hoped that a scorched earth policy might win him a victory. It was early summer and the crops were only just beginning to sprout. Every scrap of food which was moveable had been taken by Llywelyn to the mountains, every flock, every chicken, every pig. Those few Welsh whom John's army encountered seemed to have nothing. Had it seemed effective they would have been tortured but as this was felt to be an unsatisfactory policy for a liberating army bribery was tried instead. But not even bribery produced supplies and soon the army was eating the horses. To pursue Llywelyn into the mountains would not merely be foolish, it would be impossible. Sullenly John ordered the retreat.

But in the autumn, when the Welsh must be there to harvest the crops or themselves starve in the coming winter, John and his army came back. This time they had brought extra supplies and could also live off the land. They stormed across until they were on the Menai Straits. They burnt Bangor cathedral. The Bishop himself was captured and only set free on a payment of two hundred hawks. The devastation was appalling. Llywelyn looked at it and groaned. Somehow he must buy time.

The price was high and that there were terms at all was only because his wife Joan, John's own daughter, was the mediator. But it cost twenty thousand head of cattle, enough to deplete the herds for years, and all the land west of the Conwy river.

These were bitter years for Wales. Determined that there should be no revival of Welsh nationalism, John gave a free hand to the barons who held castles in Wales. These were cruel times in which human life and suffering was held to be of little account. But the activities of Robert Vipont in Powys, who hanged a seven-year-old child as a hostage, bred a steady hatred. And Fawkes de Beaute, a typical baron of the time, oppressed all those around Aberystwyth where his castle was. Fawkes would meet his nemesis in 1216 but that time was far ahead. Apart from his oppression and cruelties, his presence at this strategic spot helped to split Wales and retard its unification.
In 1212 there was another burst of fighting in Wales. In central and west Wales there were local risings in which newly-built castles were attacked. Llywelyn was in England at the time, but he returned and threw in his lot with the dissidents. John hastily assembled an army at Chester and prepared to teach Llywelyn a final lesson. But the attack was abortive. John realized his English barons were on the point of rebellion behind him and it would be unwise to absent himself from London. He allowed his fleet to harass the north Wales coast but then decided to accept the

mediation of the Pope in this dispute. He was in fact now so enthusiastic to have Llywelyn as a friend that he was ready to overlook the fact that the Welsh were virtually in open rebellion.

But Llywelyn was as great an opportunist as John and did not suffer from the English king's periodic bouts of lassitude. He realized that in England a new form of government was emerging – government by consent. It was still far removed from democracy but it took a tentative step towards it. The barons required the monarch to take note of their wishes, that was all Llywelyn, sensing the strength of the opposition to John, decided to declare his allegiance to these rebel barons. It was not an easy decision to take for John was by no means beaten. However, when John was preoccupied by his troubles at home Llywelyn swiftly raised a Welsh army and captured the royal castles in Wales. It was an impressive total: Cardigan, Carmarthen, Kidwelly, Llanstephan, and Cilgerran were the most important. Then, as an equal, Llywelyn joined the barons at Runnymede and obtained recognition and guarantees for Wales. Llywelyn was not so naive as to think that these hard-won gains could not be lost as quickly as they had been won, nor that John, as soon as he saw an opportunity, would not endeavour to regain absolute power. However, in the meantime Llywelyn built on this new unity of Wales and summoned a Council of Princes. He made some strange allies. One of them was Reginald de Braose, holder of Builth castle, who married his daughter. The Braose family, already mentioned, were immensely powerful and often, but not always, extremely unpopular. One of them, Giles, was now Bishop of Hereford. Yet another of Llywelyn's daughters married Ralph Mortimer. The Mortimers of Wigmore were Marcher barons but their connection with Wales would become so close, through marriages, that they would become almost as Welsh as the Welsh.

John died in 1216 and was followed by Henry III. As Henry III was an infant the real power lay with William Marshall, first the father then the son of the same name. They held Chepstow castle, which they greatly strengthened. Both Marshalls were determined that the royal power which John had come close to losing altogether should stay with the King. The latter would rule according to the terms of Magna Carta but there was now a split between those barons who wished for further baronial power, and those who were prepared to support the infant King. Among the latter was Reginald de Braose.

This, of course, brought de Braose into conflict with Llywelyn, who wished for even greater independence from the King of England. Llywelyn sprang into action, captured Builth and overran the lands almost as far as Chepstow. Here he stopped; his quarrel was not with the powerful English but with his subject barons who wished to change their allegiance. Neither did William Marshall want war with Wales at that moment.

But the uneasy peace was shattered when the younger William Marshall succeeded his father in 1219. Once more Llywelyn heard rumblings of discontent; once more he launched a punitive raid. Castles such as Narberth and Gwys, which were focal points of discontent, were completely flattened. Haverfordwest, a more formidable proposition, was burnt. Fighting was widespread. William Marshall was gradually drawn into it, relieving his supporters, retaking their castles, and assuring them of his support provided they looked to England and not Gwynedd for the rules of government.

Llywelyn showed himself the master of the swift raid. Marshall might eventually recapture the castles and barter back the hostages but it was clear that in the long run Welsh princes must look to Llywelyn for direction, not to England. William de Braose was captured at Builth and taken into Llywelyn's own court. Returning unexpectedly one day, Llywelyn found him in compromising circumstances with Joan, his wife. Within minutes young William had lost his head.

Llywelyn was as skilful a diplomat as he was on the battlefield. When he saw a chance to turn an enemy into an ally he never missed it. When eventually William Marshall died, out of favour in his declining years, Llywelyn quickly made friends with his brother Richard Marshall. Marshall was Earl of Pembroke, but owing to being out of favour with Henry III had lost Pembroke. He was a useful ally. Together the two captured the strong castles of Pembroke and Abergavenny. In 1233 Henry III took a strong army into Wales to recapture these and other strongholds. At Grosmont castle, Gwent, the royal army settled down for the night, planning its activities for the morrow. In general, war was conducted in a conventional manner in the Middle Ages. Fighting was a daytime activity, although a castle might perhaps be invaded by a climber like Morgan (of Cardiff) at night. Night fighting is highly uncertain and unpredictable: it is all too easy to attack your own men by mistake.

But there was no mistake this time. On to the sleepy English army burst a torrent of wild Welshmen. By the time Henry's army had roused itself, a good proportion had been slaughtered or wounded by the Welsh. Then the Welsh were gone. It was a typical Llywelyn attack, swift, unexpected, decisive. Llywelyn died in 1240, crippled and worn out, but not before he had made his last diplomatic move. Independence from England was perhaps impossible, but Welsh unity was not. Henceforth Wales would support England in her foreign ventures and England would give Wales her due recognition as a vassal and an ally. The son of Llywelyn, David, was half English and, through his mother, of the royal English line. In support, Llywelyn had married his daughters to the great Marcher families, the Braoses, the Mortimers and the Chesters. No man could do more. He retired to a monastery and died. But within a few years his vision was forgotten and his achievements swept away.

Llywelyn's battles were mainly for castles. His difficulties were immense. Anyone launching an army, in any age, has formidable problems and in the Middle Ages logistics was the greatest hazard. The armies of Henry I, Henry II and King John set off into Wales with high hopes. They were partly composed of professional mercenary soldiers but soldiers need food, weapons and pay; provided these are forthcoming they will normally stay in the field. If conditions become too bad, and they find themselves exposed to relentless rain as often happened in Wales, they may demur. The rest of the armies would be made up of knights paying for their land with military service. The obligation was forty days a year and therefore when the forty days were up they expected to go home. A long campaign or a long siege was thus impossible.

But Llywelyn's problems were greater than those of the English kings. He could only bring his supporters into the field of battle by leadership. He could provide them with little food or pay. When they successfully stormed castles, that supplied his troops with food, arms and a base, but they could not stay long. There was a nagging fear in the mind of any Welshman far from home that his neighbour might be raiding his flocks, killing his family, or destroying his house. The most effective spur Llywelyn could give to men's loyalty was to win battles. No one can win every battle, take every casde. That Llywelyn achieved so much with so little, against so many handicaps, is a miracle.

Chapter 7

THE BATTLES OF LLYWELYN THE LAST

Llywelyn left two sons. The elder was Griffith, a man who believed in complete independence for Wales, which he thought might be achieved if enough concessions and guarantees were given to Henry III, who was his uncle. The other was David, a mild man, who considered that endless struggles with England would lead nowhere, and the best hope for Wales was to accept vassal status with allegiance to the English crown; a Wales tom by exhausting wars against an adversary with greater resources seemed to him to be a Wales which would eventually disintegrate in spite of his father's great efforts. Griffith had rebelled against Llywelyn over what he felt should be the policy for Wales and Llywelyn, by a subterfuge, had had him arrested and imprisoned at Criccieth. Griffith remained incarcerated at Criccieth for six years.

When David succeeded to the throne it was obvious that Griffith had enough supporters to tear Wales apart. He was supported not only by Powys but by a number of Marcher lords who felt that Gwynedd was all too powerful and needed putting down. Civil war loomed. Henry III took an army to Chester partly to reconcile the brothers but partly to show that, independence movements were likely to involve heavy fighting. As Griffith was still in Criccieth, from which David had not released him, the discussions on reconciliation were somewhat one-sided. All that happened was that David swore allegiance to Henry III and Griffith was transferred to the Tower of London, in company with some other Welsh hostages. In 1244 Griffith tried to escape from the" Tower on a rope made of sheets and tapestries; it broke and he was killed in the fall. David, sensing the effect this would have on Welsh feeling, now decided to defy Henry himself and to identify more closely with his late brother's policy. Realizing the effect this policy would have on England he called out the Welsh army, and prepared for war.

In consequence, Henry III took an army to Wales in the summer of 1245, following the traditional invasion route of the north until he came to Deganwy. David did not oppose him but waited and watched. Henry III stayed at Deganwy for two months, strengthening the castle with his army camped around. They were harassed by the Welsh but could not be dislodged. One day an Irish ship carrying food and wine ran aground close to the castle. The Welsh, who were also desperate for food, realized it was within their reach as well as that of the English army. A bloody battle developed which the Welsh won. Atrocities were now committed by both sides. At the end of the summer Henry retired, having won no significant victory, and with the certain knowledge that the whole campaign must be fought again the next year. He had ravaged north Wales, but otherwise accomplished nothing. The following spring David died.

It seemed that north Wales had never known such misery But, as we have seen before, Wales often finds salvation just when its fortunes seem to be at their lowest ebb. They could not have been much worse at this time.

The first and greatest problem was there was no clearly distinct candidate for the vacant throne. Once this was satisfactorily filled there would still be other problems, such as the disappointed supporters of rival claimants, the economic misery resulting from the recent conflict, the thorny problem of relations with the English king and, not least, the endless supply of trouble-makers who thrived on any form of anarchy and wished it to continue. The last were virtually a criminal element. Wales had always had an undue proportion of such liabilities. They were the outcome of the Norman policy of two hundred years before when turbulent Norman adventurers were encouraged to find land for themselves in Wales. Such a policy kept potential malcontents busy outside England and also caused so much disruption in Wales that unity was handicapped. Some of these turbulent warriors were an embarrassment to the great Marcher lords, the. Earls of Chester, Shrewsbury and Gloucester, for they delighted to play off one against the other.

The strongest candidates for the throne, in title if not resources, were the sons of Griffith (the man who had died while trying to escape from the Tower of London). They were Owen, known as Red Owen, and Llywelyn. There was another son, David, who was not considered near enough to have any real claim. Needless to say he too became involved, with appalling consequences. For the time being Wales was divided between Llywelyn and Owen. Then there was Ralph Mortimer and, after he died, his son Roger. Gladys, the daughter of Llywelyn ap Iorweth and Joan (daughter of King John) had, after the death of her first husband, married Ralph Mortimer of Wigmore Castle. Ralph Mortimer there-fore claimed the throne by right of his wife, who was the nearest living relative to Llywelyn ap Iorweth. Their son Roger married Maud de Braose who was the daughter of that William de Braose caught in compromising circumstances with Llywelyn's wife. There was also another claimant to Welsh lands, though not the title. It was Edward, son of King Henry III. His claim was shadowy in the extreme. When Griffith was in prison at Criccieth his wife Senena had gone to Henry III and pleaded for help to obtain her husband's release. Henry had agreed to see that the rival claims were heard in a Welsh court and in gratitude for this – which never happened – Senena was to pay a large annual tribute. However, when Henry arrived in Wales he was persuaded by David to change his mind and incarcerate the unfortunate Griffith in the Tower. At this moment Henry decided that in view of the tribute he had been promised by Senena he should now take a piece of land as a reward for not opposing the claims of Griffith's eldest son. The land he took had originally been Llywelyn's and he granted it to his own son, Prince Edward, then aged eight. The lands were known as the Four Cantreds (districts). They extended from Conway to Chester and were mainly good agricultural areas. So for the time all was settled. Wales was still in a very troubled state, partly from the ruinous wars and devastation and partly from a succession of bad years with dry springs and wet autumns. And although the north seemed to be approaching stability again the rest of Wales was torn by ferocious blood feuds and savage raids which led to even more vicious reprisals. However, at first it seemed that Wales might now be proceeding to more settled times. The north was at last stabilized; prosperity began to return. The new King was popular. The only people who appeared dissatisfied with the state of affairs were his brothers Owen and David. They raised a sudden rebellion which was just as quickly suppressed. Owen was caught and imprisoned but David managed to escape to England. The fact that he would subsequently spend a considerable portion of his life as a guest of the English court would be of significance later.

Llywelyn had succeeded David in 1246. By 1255 he had established himself so well, and had such charm in addition, that he was regarded with favour all over Wales. It seemed as though the dream of Llywelyn Fawr might now be realized, and Welsh unity at last become a reality. Llywelyn had no wish to break away from the English crown. He saw himself and Wales as part of that feudal structure in which mutual dependence and mutual benefit required each person to know his place in the hierarchy. And just as Llywelyn saw himself as a vassal of the English crown, he saw his own princes as subordinate to him.

This pleasant dream was shattered when at the age of sixteen Prince Edward was appointed to the Earldom of Chester which had fallen vacant. Inevitably the young prince wished to visit his new domains and exercise some control over the Four Cantreds, which had changed little since they had formed part of the Kingdom of Gwynedd. Unfortunately his instrument there was Geoffrey Langley, a man who had made himself detested in England and Scotland but who retained royal favour because he was expert at raising money by taxation and fines. The wretched inhabitants of the Four Cantreds groaned under his extortions and the brutality with which the mercenary soldiers backed his decrees. Desperate for remedy they took their grievances to Llywelyn, begging him to free them. Llywelyn knew very well that the right course was to make some representation to Henry III.

However, Henry III was too much taken up with foreign favourites and events in France to care much what happened in Wales, as Llywelyn knew. If he thought about Wales at all, it was probably to approve of what his son was doing. And as soon as he settled down to his inheritance at Chester, Prince Edward decided to do even more than allow the Four Cantreds to be administered harshly. He decided to extend English power through to Cardigan and Carmarthen by making Patrick Chaworth, of Kidwelly Castle, the Steward of Carmarthen. This could hardly be tolerated by Llywelyn who was already bitter and resentful about the loss of the Four Cantreds. Although he knew it could lead to nothing but ultimate disaster, Llywelyn issued the call to arms. It evoked a joyous and whole-hearted response. Llywelyn marched through the Four Cantreds and came close to Chester. Yet another intermittent war had begun. In the next ten years very little went wrong for Llywelyn. Carmarthen and Cardigan were restored to the Welsh, Patrick Chaworth killed, the Mortimers ousted from the strategic castle at Builth, and even in south Wales Llywelyn was seen as a symbol of liberty. Young Edward was unable to cope with warfare on this scale. He managed to produce a strong force of Gascon mercenaries but after initial successes this army was driven out of north Wales and back into Chester. Llywelyn's victory was not complete for there were still enemy outposts he could not conquer. Deganwy was in English hands, as was Dyserth (near Prestatyn) and Dinas Bran. Dinas Bran is a peak near Llangollen which has been fortified from early times. It is possible to walk to the top of this eagle's nest if you have time and it is easy to see why it resisted conquest. There are many weird legends attached to Dinas Bran, any of which seems entirely credible when you stand in the ruins. One is that an eagle used to breed there every year; another is that it had been the scene of supernatural events. It must have seemed an isolated spot when it was held for Edward by Griffith of Bromfield, when the rest of Wales seemed in Welsh hands entirely. As always there were outposts held by both sides. One was Dynevor, which was the focal point of Llywelyn's administration of the south. It was besieged by Rees the Little, assisted by troops from Henry III. But at a critical moment in the siege Llywelyn appeared with a relieving force. A tremendous battle ensued but Llywelyn was the victor. Dynevor will appear later in this narrative in another dramatic campaign. Dynever is now open to the public during the summer months, but check the times on 01558 823902 before setting out, as they may vary.

As the war progressed, more and more troops were drawn into it. Llywelyn was said to have an army of thirty thousand foot and five hundred knights. But more than anything the war seems to have contributed to the development of Welsh archery. Both sides used bowmen extensively and it was the bow which made the penetration of mountain valleys so dangerous. From concealed vantage points, usually enjoying the benefit of superior elevation and cover, the bowmen could take a heavy toll of anyone toiling along the passes. Henry took an army to Chester in 1257 where he was met by Llywelyn. Llywelyn offered to make peace on condition that the status quo would be restored, and that Prince Edward be removed to another area. It was all too clear that the personal antagonism which was going to embitter the relationship between Llywelyn and Prince Edward was already well-established. Henry decided to treat Llywelyn simply as a rebel and defeat him. Once more the campaign roads were trodden. Henry's army ravaged the Cantreds and went on to relieve Deganwy. But it was an empty triumph. He dared not take the war into the mountains, and there was no food for an army in the countryside they had once traversed. As the army retraced its steps the Welsh bowmen took a steady toll.

In 1263 Henry was already in the dire trouble that would lead to the rebellion of Simon de Montfort. Llywelyn was able to turn this to good advantage by capturing Dyserth, Deganwy and Mold. Noting that in England Simon de Mont-fort was heading a baronial revolt against the arbitrary government of Henry III, Llywelyn decided that friendly moves would be opportune. With men to spare he was able to lend bowmen to de Montfort and these harassed King Henry's army on its march to Lewes. The battle which took place at Lewes on 14 May 1264 resulted in a victory for de Montfort and the capture of Henry III and Prince Edward. But a year later all was changed at Evesham. Roger Mortimer had never been in sympathy with the other barons, and when Prince Edward slipped away from a hunting party it was with the Mortimers of Wigmore that he found refuge. The Earl of Gloucester had changed sides and Henry was restored to power in the bloody battle of Evesham on 4 August 1265. Welsh archers trying to make their escape from Simon's defeated army were slaughtered in their hundreds on that day. But, symbolical of the times, the Earl of Gloucester was ready to change sides again a year later and there was still much opposition to Henry in the Marches. In 1267, after yet another English army had tramped its way into Wales, peace was made between Llywelyn and

Henry III in which the Welsh Prince kept the Four Cantreds, was acknowledged Prince of Wales, but paid 30,000 marks as an indemnity.

There was peace. Prince Edward went abroad on a Crusade, Henry was worn out with his struggles, and it was clear that rule by Llywelyn was accepted in Wales. But in 1272 Henry III died.

From the beginning matters began to go wrong between Edward, now Edward I, and Llywelyn. Already they disliked each other. Llywelyn was summoned to Westminster to do fealty: he did not appear. He was summoned again, and again. He said he doubted his personal safety and demanded hostages, but these were not sent. Even so, reconciliation might still have been made. But what made it no longer possible was Llywelyn's decision to marry Simon de Mont- fort's daughter. Before he could do so his unfortunate bride, named Eleanor, was captured at sea by merchantmen who handed her over to Edward.

Edward could, of course, have made a supreme gesture of conciliation and sent her to Llywelyn. But like so many wise and diplomatic steps it was prevented by suspicion and earlier bitter conflict. Instead he said he would send her to Wales if Llywelyn would go to London, with no guarantees, Llywelyn refused and both sides prepared for war.

There had been hard and capable campaigners in Wales before but none, not even Harold, with the determination of Edward I. He took an army of four divisions to Wales; he himself went to Chester, Mortimer went through Shrewsbury to Montgomery, the Earl of Hereford marched to Brecon and the Earl of Lancaster to Deheubarth. Against this massive assault the southern areas could not hold out long and when south Wales had capitulated the Earl of Lancaster began building a new more formidable castle at Aberystwyth. The south was now strategically cut off from the north. In the north Edward's army rolled relentlessly forward. At Basingwerk Edward was joined by David, Llywelyn's younger brother, who had spent long years in England but still had aspirations to rule part of Wales. For his treachery he was promised half of Snowdon. Meanwhile Edward's fleet destroyed the standing com in Anglesey. Elsewhere in Wales com had been left in the fields because the harvesters were all absent at war. Edward had a stranglehold on Wales.

Peace was signed in the Treaty of Rhuddlan, on 10 November 1277. The terms were severe; one of them was that Llywelyn would pay an indemnity of 50,000 marks. Edward's supporters were given castles at key points. Even the treacherous David received Denbigh which was in the centre of the Four Cantreds and controlled the Clwyd vale. Llywelyn then married Eleanor in Worcester Cathedral. To anyone who did not know Wales it would have appeared that all was over. But, of course, it was not.

Grievances were soon widespread. Even David found his holding at Denbigh subject to various irritating restrictions. Many of the complaints were due to the fact that the administrators neither knew, nor cared to learn, local customs. Rebellion was five years brewing but when it came it spread almost immediately through the length and breadth of Wales. David gave vent to his feelings by assaulting Hawarden castle and slaughtering the garrison. Militarily it was a fine achievement to capture Hawarden in so short a time, but that is the best you can say of this battle. He then besieged Flint and Rhuddlan which offered sterner resistance. Word of the revolt was sent to Edward who lost no time in calling out a vast army. As before he sent his fleet around by sea as he pushed forward, driving David's army away from Flint and Rhuddlan. Negotiations began while both Llywelyn and Edward kept their armies busy and ready for the next move. Unlike most campaigns this was prolonged into the winter. In November Edward sent a mixed force to cross the Menai and land at Caernarvon. They were intercepted at Moel y Don and driven back into the water. With the situation stabilized temporarily, although Edward had no intention of calling off the campaign, Llywelyn conducted a lightning tour of the southern districts. On 11 December, near Builth, he was killed by a man-at-arms, Adam of Frankton – who came across him by chance and was unaware who he was fighting.

It was not quite the end of the war. David announced that he was now Prince of Wales and resistance would continue. But with a starving army he could not last and was soon betrayed and captured. Edward despised him as a man who had betrayed both sides, first his English friends from the time of his exile (he was made an English baron), then his brother in the hour of need. He was executed, as many of his peers were in the Middle Ages. He was dragged through the streets of Shrewsbury then hanged, drawn and quartered. It was a vile form of death but one which thousands of others, innocent and guilty, suffered at the time and for centuries later.

Some mystery surrounds Llywelyn's death. The details of his last day involve the battle of Orewin Bridge. Llywelyn had come south with a force of unknown size but probably less than one thousand. He gained more supporters in Brecon and was hoping to do the same at Builth Castle. Although today there is not a single stone on the earthworks of Builth Castle the visitor will see at a glance its immense strategic significance. It has, of course, been mentioned many times during this book. The importance of Builth was not lost on the Marcher lords and two of them, John Giffard and Edmund Mortimer, had set off to isolate it with a body of troops raised from Shropshire. Llywelyn decided to block their progress at Orewin Bridge, over the Irfon, a tributary of the Wye. His army had been waiting for the English force for some time on the steep hill on the far side, with a ready array of spearmen (this was an army from north Wales where the spear was still a principal weapon). From here they could watch and rapidly annihilate any force trying to cross the bridge. Llywelyn was not with them as he had gone off to rally some local leaders whose support was thought to be wavering; this may or may not have been the garrison at Builth. Had his troops stayed in their allotted position it would have boded ill for the Shropshire force. However, the inevitable streak of treachery had appeared and a local inhabitant had revealed to the Marcher army a ford upstream. A strong infantry force had crossed this during the night and at dawn fell on the Welsh army. The absence of Llywelyn now proved disastrous for there was no overall direction of this newly-recruited army, made up of independent groups which took orders from no one but their own local chieftain. All turned to confront the flank attack, leaving the bridge unguarded. It was the result the Marchers had planned and hoped for but scarcely expected. They crossed the unguarded bridge with cavalry whose advance was covered by archers. To use archers in this way to ease the way for cavalry was a form of warfare which was rarely employed in the Middle Ages; in subsequent centuries artillery would invariably 'soften up' the opposition (or try to) before any advance. The Marcher force swept up the hill and cut into the spearmen who were now thoroughly disorganized. In such circumstances it was the Welsh custom to disappear from the scene but regroup later, perhaps the next day. Therefore they fought for a while here and there and then began to flee. A messenger had been sent to Llywelyn, who some say was at Builth, trying to enlist the garrison's support. It was believed that in order to approach Builth secretly he had ridden on a horse which had had its shoes reversed, thus leaving misleading tracks. This story seems improbable. However as he came towards the battlefield he encountered an English esquire, Adam de Frankton. Adam (also called by some chroniclers Stephen!) is said to have come from Shropshire or Cheshire; in fact he came from Frankton in Warwickshire. Seeing a Welsh horseman on the outskirts of the battle he dashed up to him and killed him, quite unaware of whom he was attacking. Doubtless Llywelyn had himself killed dozens of men-at-arms in battle but this time he was unlucky. His head was taken to London to be placed on Tower Bridge. This again was a medieval custom. His body was buried at Abbey Cwmhir. There is a monument by the road at Cilmeri which says: 'Near this spot was killed our Prince Llywelyn 1282.'

Perhaps the best tribute to Llywelyn was that given by Edward I by the size of the programme for building Welsh castles. They had already been begun in 1282. Curiously enough, one of the most formidable Welsh castles, Caerphilly (Caerfili) was not built by Edward at all but by Gilbert de Clare, but it probably served as a model. Caerphilly was begun in 1268 and twice destroyed by Llywelyn before it was finally completed.

The great castles of the north are the pride of Wales, partly because they are a tribute to Welsh military resilience and partly because they are edifices of remarkable beauty. Builth was once the strongest, apparently exactly fitted to its position on the hill. But every stone of Builth above ground has now disappeared. In the same year that the reconstruction of Builth was begun so also was that at Flint, Rhuddlan and Aberystwyth. All three of these could be supplied from the sea, although at Rhuddlan the River Clwyd had to be diverted for the purpose. Rhuddlan subsequently became very decayed and overgrown, but has now been well restored and is a mecca for tourists. Flint is also badly ruined but no one visiting it could fail to appreciate its former strength. Aberystwyth is also but a shadow of its former greatness but no one who has read this book will omit to visit that site which was so often fought for. These first four castles would have cost about £1,500,000 each at present-day values. While they were being built, by drawing skilled labour from all over England and Wales, Edward was also strengthening and rebuilding many smaller castles. The size of this project staggers the imagination, particularly as most of the time Edward was engaged in difficult and expensive wars in Scotland and France. The second chain of large Welsh castles was Conwy, Caernarvon and Harlech. They were begun before the others were completed and Beaumaris was soon added to their number. Some took many years and were never finished according to the original specifications. Conwy, Caernarvon, Harlech and Beaumaris cannot have cost less than the equivalent of about £3 million each. The whole of Europe was scoured to find the right quantity and quality of designers and masons for these castles.

They represented, and still represent, the ultimate in sophisticated castle building. They embody every device which had been learnt in over two thousand years of fortification and three hundred years of castle-building. Early castles had all been of linear pattern. The aim had been to make the attacker fight first of all at the barbican (outer defence protecting the main gate), then through the gatehouse itself, protected by its drawbridge, portcullis and machicolations. After the first gatehouse the attacker would have to fight his way through another bailey, into another gatehouse and then into another bailey. Finally, when he reached the centre he would come to the keep, sometimes built on the original motte. He might, if he were very lucky, break in through the sides, but in general, the gatehouses, difficult through they were, offered an easier way. Conway and Caernarvon are both linear castles and both were linked to extremely formidable town walls, each studded with towers as strong as many small castles.

Many of the subtleties of these castles are no longer obvious. For example, most men carried a shield on the left arm and a sword on the right. If you built a passage which made the attacker turn right, this meant at the moment he turned his sword arm was at a disadvantage. This device was used in horizontal passageways but even more effectively on spiral staircases. It will be noticed that most, though not all, staircases wind away to the right, putting the ascender constantly at a disadvantage, for he would often strike his sword arm on the central pillar. But in each castle you will find one or more staircases which wind in the opposite direction. These were made so that if the castle owner lost a floor, he would know the best place to try to regain it; this would be the staircase which would turn to the left instead of the right.

At Beaumaris and Harlech the visitor will note that if an attacker broke through one wall he would find himself at a great disadvantage owing to the narrowness of the space in which he was now operating. There would be no room to use a battering ram and every move he made would be threatened from a surrounding building. There were no inner ramparts, so if he climbed to the top of the wall he made a perfect target for an archer operating from the next line of defence. A normal method of attacking castles was by mining underneath the walls. At Beaumaris and Harlech this would have been impossible, for the workings would have been flooded from the surrounding water (at the time of its construction Harlech was on the sea). With the other castles, if water did not make mining impossible, rock certainly did. Before the days of pneumatic drills and easily controllable explosives, the only method of splitting rock was to heat it by building fires on it, then suddenly cooling it with cold water. Digging out the foundations by this method was a tedious and laborious process; mining would have been impossible.

One of the most concise, yet informative, accounts of Edward's castle-building in Wales was the late J. Goronwy Edwards's Sir John Rhys Memorial Lecture delivered at the British Academy in 1944. It was subsequently published by the Oxford University Press. 1944, when missiles were raining on London, was scarcely a time for quiet contemplation of accounts of building procedure some seven hundred and fifty years before, one might think; perhaps, however, it was appropriate.

Although Edward was lavish with labour and resources in building the castles, the design of each was partly aimed at economizing in manpower in the garrison. Harlech, as we see later, could be defended with forty men. It is a military axiom that one defender is equal to three attackers, but in these castles the defenders could be outnumbered by more than ten to one and still be on equal terms. The advantage of a small garrison is that it is economical on food supplies, and in a long siege this is all important. Another factor which makes a small-size garrison popular is that it does not dissipate manpower resources. In English castles, especially those in the Marches, garrisons were provided by what was known as 'castle-guard'. Castle-guard was the legal requirement for a man or his family to do a tour of duty on watch in the local castle. Sometimes a family served at one watch-tower or parapet so long that the point became known by the family name, e.g. Blake Tower.

However, this was not possible in Wales, for to introduce a local family into, say, Aberystwyth in the early stages of the post-Edwardian era was like handing the key to a potential enemy.

In addition to the building and strengthening which went on there was considerable redistribution of ownership. For example, Dinas Bran, dominating the neighbouring town of Llangollen and overlooking vital passes, was given to the Earl of Warenne and Surrey. As he held many other castles in different parts of the country he probably spent little time at Dinas Bran, but the fact that he was responsible for it and could, if needs be, muster large resources, made it a powerful stronghold. However, as we have seen before, the Welsh had a remarkable way of absorbing the occupying power into their own system, often by marriage. Occasionally the former enemy would become an ally in the next rebellion. Sometimes these great castle-holders used their powerful positions to ferment rebellions on their own account.

Henry de Lacy, Earl of Lincoln, was granted Denbigh castle after it was taken from David, Llywelyn's brother. At the time it was probably no more than a wooden castle, but under de Lacy it was not only built into a very strong castle but also linked to the town walls. Although Denbigh is now a ruin, a glance at the ground plan displayed at the entrance shows its immense former strength. There was a barbican at the front and rear, seven very strong wall towers and a gatehouse consisting of three more towers closely set together. Anyone breaking into that gatehouse was likely to have cause to regret it. Denbigh castle was, in fact, captured in 1294, long before its completion but it was retaken and the building went on. The entire construction probably took nearly forty years. De Lacy was said to have left it some time before its completion; it is believed that his eldest son fell into the castle well and was drowned. At Chirk Castle, which is one of the best preserved castles in the country and is still lived in, was Roger Mortimer. Chirk is strategically placed between the Dee and the Severn. Among its many striking features are the massive drum towers. Roger Mortimer's elder brother Edward was at Wigmore and was viewed with some suspicion as he was now the heir to the Welsh crown. Humphrey de Bohun, Earl of Hereford, came of a family which had sided with Simon de Montfort and which would join the rebellion leading to the deposition of Edward II. However, for the moment de Bohun was much more concerned with his bitter rivalry with Gilbert de Clare, Earl of Gloucester. De Bohun and de Clare occasionally fought pitched battles over disputed territory. The Welsh observed these jealousies, feuds and discords among the Marchers and waited their opportunity. De Clare had at one time supported Llywelyn the Last. The most encouraging sign for a more stable future was the birth of Edward I's son at Caernarvon in 1284. He was to be the Prince of Wales, and as such the Welsh took him to their hearts. Unfortunately, when he became king he had a disastrous reign.

But even in the immediate aftermath of the death of Llywelyn it was obvious that Wales was not going to settle down without further widespread fighting. The first person to show his disenchantment was Rees ap Meredith, Prince of South Wales. He felt that as he had assisted Edward against Llywelyn he should be treated with proper courtesy; however, now that Edward had gone over to France, his administrators paid scant heed to Rees's special position and instead Rees found his land and his judicial power encroached on. Suddenly his anger flared up. He captured Dynevor, Drysllwyn, Llandovery and Carreg Cennen castles, and sent the new administrators packing.

Dynevor, Drysllwyn and Carreg Cennen are five miles apart from each other, along the Towy. The task of recapturing the formidable trio was given to Edmund of Cornwall, who was acting as regent while Edward was in France. Drysllwyn was his first task, but it took him twenty-one days. The peaceful character of the hill on which it stands by the River Towy contrasts sharply with what we know of the events of June 1287. Edmund brought up 1100 men, with whom he surrounded the castle, but his main asset was a piece of siege machinery known as a trebuchet. Siege engines were a form of giant catapult, sometimes worked by a bowstring with plaited human hair (which was very tensile), sometimes by a counterpoise. This trebuchet was worked by a counterpoise. Such machines could launch a 500 lb. piece of stone with astonishing accuracy. This one must have been massive, for it required forty oxen to draw it over smooth ground but sixty when the going was harder. It was protected against attack by an escort of twenty horsemen and four hundred and eighty foot soldiers. For this siege 480 huge stones were brought up by a packhorse train. There were also other smaller machines in use and also the inevitable miners burrowing away beneath the castle walls. The miners were successful a little too soon, for they brought down a wall unexpectedly and as it fell outwards it killed a number of knights who were standing close to the walls. Towards the end of the siege Rees escaped through a postern but did not, as might have been expected, fall back on Dynevor or Carreg Cennen. (The latter looks absolutely impregnable although in practice it proved not to be so.) Instead he moved straight to Newcastle Emlyn. He captured this by surprise. Newcastle Emlyn is nowadays in a very ruined state but anyone visiting it can see from its position virtually surrounded by water that it would be very difficult to capture. And so it proved to be. Not until the following January did it fall. By then the elusive Rees had left it and was on his way to Ireland. He reappeared in 1290 when local discontent was once more seething but this time the local forces were more organized and he was captured without any dramatic sieges.

The next rising was more serious and even affected Edward I himself. The cost of all these castles and the campaigns in Wales, Scotland and France, led to the imposition of ever increasing taxes. These were particularly resented in Dyfed where people thought that Pembroke and Carmarthen were getting off too lightly. Although Edward had tried to win over Welsh feeling by preserving much Celtic law (instead of introducing the Norman form), and also by appointing many Welsh administrators, this had not been wholly successful. There was still much of the inter-area jealousy and rivalry which we have seen before ruining Welsh co-operation. Maelgwyn suddenly led a revolt in Dyfed. Almost simultaneously one broke out in Glamorgan and caused Gilbert de Clare to leave the district immediately. Denbigh castle came under siege. And worst of all, a man named Madoc, who said he was a son of Llywelyn the Last, raised an army of followers at Caemavon, attacked the castle which was still incomplete, and burnt the town. Suddenly it seemed as though, in spite of conquests and castles, Wales was lost and would have to be re-conquered. For what had begun as a few spontaneous outbreaks of defiance had now become a general insurrection with an organized army. Edward had planned to be in France in the autumn but instead he had to stay and raise more soldiers, and demand more taxes to pay them. Denbigh was lost and when de Lacy tried to retake it his relieving army was swept away. Edward was unable to begin his own campaign until the winter was setting in. He encountered strong resistance when crossing the Conwy and when he reached the castle found himself beleaguered by a flooded river. Apparently he sat in the banqueting hall eating a Christmas dinner of salt meat and stale bread and not much of either. The outcome of the campaign was inevitable for when the river level went down Edward was relieved; however it had been an unnerving experience and a warning of the precariousness of the position of any conqueror in north Wales.

An interesting battle took place at Conway on 22 January 1295. The Earl of Warwick was approaching Conway with a relieving force brought from Rhuddlan. He knew, from the inevitable agents, that the Welsh army was on a hill in an open space with woods on each flank. If attacked by superior forces they planned to melt away into the woods. However, by a long night-march Warwick came up so quickly that he surprised the insurgents at dawn. He sent two arms of cavalry along the flanks to cut off their retirement into the woods or to hinder it so much that it would prove a disastrous manoeuvre – then prepared to charge and destroy the centre. The Welsh, seeing what was intended, planted their spears in the earth with the points facing outwards at 45 degrees. It was a traditional form of warfare, and the shout 'Prepare to receive cavalry' would be heard by pikemen on battlefields for centuries to come. However on this occasion Warwick cunningly interspersed his own archers between the charging horses. The term 'a charge' gives the misleading impression that horses went into battle at the gallop: in fact it was usually at a walk or slow trot so the archers would have no difficulty in keeping up with them. The Welsh did not ask for quarter but fought it to the end; in consequence this was a very bloody battlefield. Madoc was captured and incarcerated in the Tower of London but whether he was taken at Conway or later is not clear. Some believe that he escaped at Conway but was able to harass the retreating English army back into Shropshire where finally he was captured in a battle somewhere between Oswestry and Shrewsbury. But the last part is mere tradition.

Chapter 8

THE BATTLES OF OWAIN GLYNDWR

In the hundred years which followed the defeat of Madoc, Welsh energy and adventure took a different course from the one it had followed previously. Edward II, though an in-competent and unfortunate king, had some saving graces. Among them was a desire to see justice done. In consequence he took his title of Edward of Caernarvon, Prince of Wales, very seriously, and in judicial matters in Wales ruled that the Welsh themselves should never have less than an equal say. He was, incidentally, not appointed Prince of Wales till 1301, when he was already seventeen and over six feet tall: the popular legend of his father raising his son on his shield and showing him to the assembled multitude saying 'This, my son, Edward of Caernarvon, will now be Prince of Wales' would have been physically impossible.

The fact that Edward was so proud of his title of Prince of Wales made it easier for the Welsh to accept him, to be loyal to him, and to like him. Thus when he went up to Scotland in 1314, where he met disaster at Bannockburn, five hundred Welshmen from Glamorgan were in his army and came as near as anyone to saving the day. But when there were revolts in Wales they were against local tyrants rather than English suzerainty. In his last months, when his own folly and others' treachery had lost him the throne, Edward wandered through Wales as a fugitive.

Very different was the reign of his son, Edward III. With his son, the Black Prince, he campaigned relentlessly in France. Both had large contingents of Welsh archers in their armies. At Crecy in 1346 the archers, close on five thousand in number, sent in a devastating opening volley of some 60,000 arrows on to the advancing Genoese crossbowmen and French horse. The longbow had an enormous advantage in that, in a shower, the string could be detached, wound in-side the archer's cap, and thus protected from the rain.

The moment the shower ceased it could be re-fitted – dry. The crossbowman, on the other hand, was out of action for hours once his more cumbersome weapon became wet. After this battle, the Black Prince who was Prince of Wales took the emblem of three feathers and the motto 'Ich dien' (I serve). Nor was this the only battle in which the archer was decisive. He wreaked havoc against the Scottish pikemen at the battle of Neville's Cross in the same year, and against the French again at Poitiers in 1356. Fear of the longbow swept through France. Its deadly long-range destruction made it seem an almost supernatural weapon. Prayers against it were offered in the French churches. However its destructive powers never seemed to have any effect on French military thought. French knights went to battle as before, heavily encumbered and scarcely mobile. At Agincourt in 1415 they were once more decisively, overwhelmingly defeated. The army against them was a quarter of their numbers, and tired, cold and hungry as well. But it still managed to pour out 72,000 arrows in the first appalling minute. Most of the bowmen were Welsh.

But meanwhile much had been happening in Wales. Richard II, son of the Black Prince, proved as incompetent and unlucky as Edward II had been and was eventually captured by the future Henry IV at Flint Castle. There is an extraordinary story of how, when the two met in the bailey of the castle, Richard's dog, which had previously never left his side, went up to Henry IV and put his paws on his shoulders. This was 1399. But Henry's usurpation did him little good: few kings have had such a troubled reign.

Ten years before the end of Richard's reign – in 1389 – trouble was brewing in north Wales. Reginald Grey of Ruthin was one of the most greedy landowners Wales had experienced since Norman times. He acquired lands by litigation and through simply seizing them. It was difficult for a man who had lost his lands to sue for them back in the face of an immensely powerful local tyranny. Often land was required to be forfeited on a trumped up charge of offending against the law. Many a man who had painfully saved to buy the freehold of his land was now told his title was invalid and he must pay more. The sum fixed was usually more than he possessed.

A crisis occurred over the land of a Welsh squire named Owain Glyndwr. Glyndwr was no simple, half-literate rustic, but a gentleman and a scholar; he had studied law in London and also served in the English army. When Glyndwr returned to Wales in September 1400, he realized that not only had he himself suffered injustice over his lands but that there were hundreds like him. This coincided with a wave of popular feeling in support of Richard II who had been deposed by Henry IV and put in Pontefract castle, after which he had never been heard of again. However, rumour had it that he was still alive and would soon be restored. Glyndwr's opening move was to avenge himself on Grey by burning his castle at Ruthin. Grey fled. Every man in Wales who felt he was oppressed – and there were many-flocked to join Glyndwr. Students came streaming back from London and Oxford,

Welshmen working in England, even mercenaries from France, all came to join this new leader, who was of the house of Llywelyn and who now, on the strength of it, pronounced himself Prince of North Wales. Henry decided on a swift suppression of this dangerous movement and took an army to Wales. He punished various people whom he thought had encouraged or connived at the rebellion. But he never encountered Glyndwr.

The next upsurge came in the spring of 1401. Glyndwr's nephews, Gwilym and Rees, had captured Conway in a daring surprise attack. Forty men had scaled the castle walls on Good Friday morning when the garrison were all attending divine service. Prince Henry (later Henry V) and Harry Percy (Hotspur) were sent to retake it. This was quickly accomplished and the pair went on to win another victory at Cader Idris. But they never met Glyndwr. Wherever they -or anyone else-went to find him, he was always some-where else. He would appear to encourage a local rebellion then reappear many miles away. Soon he was considered to have supernatural powers, to be able to ride on the storm or to take a different body. Henry himself decided to eliminate this dangerous threat to his own prestige. He marched his army through the country and made his headquarters at Strata Florida near Cardigan, which was the burial place of Welsh princes. He devastated the countryside. But he still did not catch Glyndwr. Instead his army was harassed by the daring Welsh guerrilla leader, who on one occasion captured valuable equipment by a sudden attack on Henry's army. Glyndwr just failed to capture Harlech. He made sudden swift raids into Shropshire, Herefordshire and Gloucester-shire. Here he was frequently assisted by Welshmen who had bought land and settled in the district. The English parliament passed statutes which said that no Welshman could buy land in such towns as Shrewsbury, Ludlow, Hereford and Gloucester and men who had Welsh tenants were made personally responsible for them. These were repressive measures but they did nothing to stop the rise of Welsh power.

In 1402 Glyndwr suddenly ceased to be a fugitive guerrilla leader and began acting like a national figure. He tried to make alliances with the Irish and Scots and he tried to negotiate a peace with England. He also gave great encouragement to Welsh culture. And he won two more battles, both very decisively. One was the battle of the Vymwy, the other was at Pilleth, sometimes known as Bryn Glas. At the Vymwy the hated Lord Grey was taken prisoner and two thousand of Henry's army were killed. At Pilleth an army under Edward Mortimer was overwhelmed and Mortimer himself taken prisoner. Subsequently Mortimer married Glyndwr's daughter; he died of starvation in the siege of Harlech Castle in 1409. The battle of Pilleth is fully described in British Battlefields: the South in this series.

Henry now directed the campaign personally. His army went into Wales along the three traditional paths, north, central and southern, and accomplished nothing. The weather was bad and, as had happened so often before, the invaders found themselves cold, wet, miserable and unable to make much headway through flooded streams and paths. The worst part of it was the wind which blew down tents with frightening violence. In that superstitious age the hostility of the elements seemed proof positive that Glyndwr had power over wind, rain and probably earthquakes.

In 1402, Prince Henry, the future Henry V, gave a taste of his future prowess by taking an army right through the centre of Wales. Although a God-fearing man, his religion did not prevent him from spreading havoc in an attempt to crush the Welsh nationalistic spirit. Glyndwr's followers seem to have been little better, for when they captured castles the occupants received little mercy. Perhaps for that reason the castles which resisted him did so with the determination normally shown by those expecting 'no quarter' if conquered. One of the most resolute was John Skidmore (or Scudamore) at Carreg Cennen, who held out for a year. Carreg Cennen, as the visitor will quickly appreciate, is a formidable, as well as a very beautiful, castle. It is completely inaccessible on one side being built on the edge of a cliff but on the other, although difficult, is not impossible. No one who enjoys visiting castles should miss Carreg Cennen.

Carmarthen endured a long siege but then fell. The town was burnt at the same time. However, Glyndwr did not hold it for long, for with a great effort the English recaptured it. This might well have seemed the end of the matter, but Glyndwr then arrived again and with the assistance of French troops once more entered into possession. Unfortunately, there is little left of Carmarthen castle today and the remains are once more besieged – this time by local government offices. Carew was another castle which came under heavy attack; by iron determination it held out.

In July 1403 the weather, which had so long been an ally of Glyndwr now became an enemy. When the Percies and the Douglases fought King Henry at the battle of Shrewsbury Glyndwr was unable to bring a Welsh contingent to his rebel allies; he was trapped by floods in Carmarthen. His presence at Shrewsbury could well have turned the scale. Instead, Henry IV was the decisive victor and Harry-Percy (Hotspur) was killed. Had Henry lost this battle the course of Welsh history would undoubtedly have been changed. As soon as he could make the journey Glyndwr brought up his army and it seemed as if there would now be a battle at Leominster. However, Glyndwr had no intention of fighting on ground not of his own choosing, particularly as the English army had a large contingent of archers from Cheshire. In consequence, as Henry came to confront him he retreated slowly over the border, hoping that Henry, flushed with victory, would follow him into Wales. Henry was much too wise to make such a move. He left him alone.

In 1404 it seemed as though the year of independent Wales had come. Glyndwr had a Welsh parliament at Dolgellau and Machynlleth and seemed to have the entire country, with the exception of those few obstinate castles, under control. Cardiff had fallen but Caernarvon and Harlech were still obstinately holding out. Coity was the scene of an epic siege and continued to resist long after it was expected to surrender.

At first there had been talk of restoring Richard II to the English throne but by 1404 all hope of his still being alive had been abandoned. In 1405 Glyndwr was planning to put Edmund Mortimer, Earl of March, on the English throne. This ambitious plan depended on his obtaining substantial help from the French, as well as the use of some Spanish mercenaries. In 1405 Prince Henry succeeded in defeating Glyndwr's army twice, once at Grosmont and then, even more decisively, at Mynydd Pwll Melyn, in Powys. And there were other reverses inflicted by the Marcher Lords.

Nevertheless, in 1406 Glyndwr was full of plans for the future. He was talking of establishing two universities in Wales. He summoned more Parliaments. Twice there were attempts to assassinate him, but these did not show declining popularity: throughout Wales he was revered.

The end came slowly. The great castles proved the stranglehold Edward I had meant them to be. Ironically, the ones which Glyndwr captured proved to be more of a liability than an asset. He made Harlech his capital and lodged his family there. It was a fatal mistake for a guerrilla leader to surrender his greatest asset, his mobility. In 1408 Harlech was beseiged by 1000 men and when the castle fell in 1409 Glyndwr's wife, daughter and four grandchildren were all captured.

Glyndwr continued to resist till 1412; he was then 58. He was offered a free pardon but preferred to live as a fugitive. He died in 1416 and is thought to have been buried in an unmarked grave in Monnington, Herefordshire. It is difficult to believe that one of his faithful followers did not take his heart back to be buried in the Wales for which he had fought so long and hard.

Few men have been so well-known yet so mysterious. He was one of the greatest guerrilla leaders but we know little of how he planned his campaigns, inspired his men, and consolidated his successes. Doubtless those who knew him best preferred to keep their knowledge to themselves lest his security be jeopardized. When he died most of them were already dead. Thus he remains as elusive to posterity as he was to his opponents.

Chapter 9

THE BATTLES OF THE CIVIL WAR

The Wars of the Roses, between the Yorkists and Lancastrians, are usually thought of as being so much an English concern that few realize that both sides depended heavily on Welsh support. When Henry V, formerly Prince Henry of Monmouth, died prematurely, his son, the heir to the English throne, was not yet one year old. Unfortunately as the boy, now Henry VI, grew up, he proved to be obstinate and foolish and at times completely insane. After a series of disasters abroad, England became split between the supporters of the House of Lancaster, to which Henry VI belonged, and the supporters of the Duke of York who would eventually put Edward IV on the throne. The Dukes of York descended from Anne Mortimer, who in turn was descended from Llywelyn the Last.

But the Lancastrians also had strong Welsh connections. Henry V's widow had married Owen Tudor, a country gentleman from Anglesey. They had two children, Edmund and Jasper. Edmund married Margaret Beaufort and they had a son. He became Henry VII of England.

The war began in 1455 and is generally considered to have been concluded by the Battle of Tewkesbury in 1471. However, Henry VII did not obtain the English throne till 1485, after the Battle of Bosworth, and the last battle was not until 1487 (Stoke Field, Nottinghamshire).

The Mortimers with their Marcher lands and their strong Welsh connection, were clearly a source of enormous strength to the Yorkists. So too was Sir William Herbert of Gwent. But if the east side of Wales was strongly Yorkist, the west side was no less staunchly Lancastrian. This line-up contributed largely to the battle of Mortimer's Cross on 2 February 1461 which was described in British Battlefields: the South in the general context of the Wars of the Roses. Mortimer's Cross is near Lucton and is where the road crosses the River Lugg. As the Yorkists had recently been heavily defeated at Wakefield it seemed inevitable that the strong mixed force of Welsh, French, Irish and Bretons would sweep aside any force which young Edward of York could put against them. But it was not to be. Although Edward was only eighteen he was one of the great tacticians of his age and it was the Lancastrian force which was routed. Owen Tudor was taken to Hereford (though some say to Haverfordwest) and beheaded in the market place. But the Welsh, of course, did not fight only in Wales or on the Welsh borders. The battle of Edgecote (Northants) in 1469 saw a surprising Yorkist victory in which 2000 Welshmen fell. Their leader, Lord Herbert, Earl of Pembroke, was executed.

Harlech castle withstood a seven-year siege by the Yorkists. The future Henry VII was said to have been in it at the time. The siege cannot have been too exacting, for Harlech could still be supplied from the sea most of the time. Only when it was completely beleaguered, and the garrison at the point of starvation, did the castellan surrender. He was Sir David ap Jevan ap Einion and he used to say that in his youth he had held a castle in France so long that every old woman in Wales had heard of it and in his old age had held a castle in Wales so long that every old woman in France had heard of it. The March of the Men of Harlech dates from this period but unfortunately no one knows what epic event it commemorates. Nor, unfortunately, do we have any record of other events of this seven-year siege.

Ultimately, as is well-known, young Henry Tudor, Earl of Richmond, landed at Haverfordwest, with a token force, in 1485. He marched through Wales gathering supporters on the way, and by his victory at Bosworth he finally united Wales and England. It was an ironic situation and it would have been interesting to know what Llywelyn ap Iorweth, and Llywelyn the Last would have thought of it The union in fact was only completed in 1535 by a Parliamentary Statute which abolished Welsh laws and customs and made the Welsh language unofficial. In this statute the Marches were divided into shires: Denbighshire, Montgomeryshire, Radnorshire, Brecknockshire and Monmouthshire. There were also changes to shires which had already been created by Edward I, i.e. Caernarvonshire, Merionethshire, Carmarthenshire, Cardiganshire and Flintshire. What is not generally realized is that all of these were the areas of a former Welsh kingdom. Brecknockshire was the former Brycheiniog, Monmouth was formerly Gwent, and Glamorgan was Morgannwg. Carmarthenshire was the old Deheubarth, Cardiganshire the old Ceredigion and Pembrokeshire was Dyfed. An arbitrary boundary was made between England and Wales which ran fairly close to Offa's Dyke. It was not a language boundary, for there were Welsh speakers on the English side of it and English speakers in some of the Welsh counties. The land east of die Wye lower than Monmouth became part of Gloucestershire. This had been a no-man's-land for centuries and had been well-trodden by Welsh raiders. Shrewsbury had once been capital of Powys but it now became the principal town of the county which also included Oswestry and Ellesmere. Wigmore was no longer the centre of a March but a declining castle in Herefordshire. In the 1972 Local Government Act many counties in England and Wales were redefined and renamed; it was said to be 'in the cause of functional effectiveness'. All the old Welsh county names were swept away and former ones substituted. This may have made the task of local government easier but it created considerable problems for the tourist. Those who earnestly make 'reforms' are often surprised when the people they are meant to benefit turn out to be not only ungrateful but actively resentful. However, the readers of this book will presumably be familiar with old, later, and current names.

Just over a hundred years after the union act, when Wales had settled down to a more peaceable mode of life than it had ever known, it was once more the scene of widespread conflict. This time the cause was the Civil War. Most people realize how deeply the Scots were involved in what is often described as the English Civil War, but few appreciate how deeply the Welsh were committed. Surprisingly, most of Wales was fervently loyal to the Royalist cause; the only parts which were sympathetic to Parliament were the ones heavily settled by Englishmen, such as Pembrokeshire. Charles I could always count on Welsh soldiers for his army. It was a pity that by this time the longbow was thought to be obsolete, having been made so by muskets, for the Welsh archers might have saved lives by winning swifter victories. The efficiency of the longbow as a weapon was not exceeded by the musket until the Napoleonic Wars, but it had long since fallen into disuse; fashion sometimes dictates military usage more than efficiency.

The course of the Civil War was complicated but we are only concerned with it where it involves Wales. However, it should be borne in mind that though most of the fighting occurred in England there was rarely a major battle in which Welshmen were not present. The first great battle was at Edgehill, Warwickshire, in 1642. Five thousand Welshmen were in the Royalist army. It was a drawn battle and Charles should have followed it by pressing on to London but he lingered and missed his opportunity. In Wales, however, his cause prospered and his supporters secured almost everything he wanted. Nevertheless, the fact that the Roundheads were firmly in possession of Pembroke and Gloucester made it very difficult for Charles to benefit from Welsh sup-port. Through 1643 and 1644 battles were lost and won by both sides, but in 1645 the Roundheads, now rightly deserving the name of Ironsides, began to gain the upper hand. The war was virtually lost for Charles when he was defeated at Naseby in June 1645 but hostilities were by no means over. In 1648 fighting flared up again although Charles was still a prisoner in Carisbrooke castle. The second phase lasted a few months only but it enabled the more fanatical Parliamentarians to press for Charles's execution. He died with great dignity on the scaffold in Whitehall in 1649.

But the war went on. Charles, Prince of Wales, later to be Charles II, inspired further resistance to Cromwell, but everything eventually ended at the battle of Worcester on 3 September 1651.
On the Welsh border the key points in the campaign were the same as they had been in all the wars throughout past centuries: they were Gloucester, Shrewsbury and Chester. Gloucester effectively blocked any excursions from south Wales and in 1643 Roundhead forces moved into Chepstow and Monmouth, thereby sealing the door even tighter. Chester was Royalist but the county of Chester was not and to make matters worse for the Royalists there was a very lively and able Roundhead commander in north Wales, Thomas Myddleton. Myddleton was known to be a Roundhead supporter, so the Royalists had promptly seized Chirk castle in his absence. Myddleton swiftly occupied Wrexham, Hawarden, Holt and Flint, and even besieged his own castle! He was driven away by an Irish army, but soon turned the tables again. Later in the war he became disgusted by the fanaticism of the Roundheads and joined the Royalists. He soon found himself besieged in Chirk which was rapidly being knocked to pieces by Roundhead artillery. However the Myddleton family retained their ownership of the castle and still live there.

In the early summer of 1645 the Royalist cause was prospering greatly in Wales. Gerard had captured Haverford-west, Cardigan, Carew Castle and Picton Castle. From this succession of victories he planned to march to relieve Chester which was virtually under siege. Then came Naseby.

Although a Roundhead victory it was no disgrace to the Royalist soldiers, only to their commanders. The Royalist infantry fought with magnificent courage and resolution; many of them were Welsh. In his hour of desperate need Charles turned once more to Wales. He was not disappointed. Large numbers of men flocked to join him. Supporting the King in this war meant offering not only your services and perhaps your life but probably your property as well. Unfortunately the honey-moon was brief. The Welsh were prepared to serve the King but only under their own leaders. Earlier in the war they had taken a violent dislike to the high-handedness of Prince Rupert and his entourage and more recently had taken exception to the Royalist General Gerard. The King replaced Gerard by Asdey but his move was too late. The Roundheads were already making inroads into former Royalist areas. Chester fell in February 1646 and Harlech castle surrendered in March 1647; its garrison numbered fifty. The conqueror of Harlech was Thomas Mytton of Halston. He was the ancestor of John Mytton, the eccentric Shropshire squire who gambled away a fortune and died at an early age owing to his extraordinary follies. Once he went duck shooting, naked, in the frost of a January night.

But it was not all loss. In 1647 General Laugharne, who had won many victories for the Roundheads, now changed sides and fought for Charles. In 1648 Wales was alight again and it seemed as though Charles once more had a chance.

But Cromwell's thoroughness had now penetrated to every corner of the Roundhead army. He appointed Horton to re-conquer Wales, and later joined him personally. Wales had experienced many ruthless campaigns but this one, in which resistance was systematically and thoroughly destroyed, was as bad as any of its predecessors. Horton defeated Laugharne at St Fagans in May 1648, a battle to which we shall return in a moment. After it Cromwell arrived in Chepstow where the town but not the castle was in Roundhead hands. The defender of Chepstow castle was Sir Nicholas Kemeys. It had already withstood an earlier siege between 1643 and 1645 and only surrendered in October of the latter year when the Royalists were already capitulating elsewhere. Its garrison at that time numbered sixty-four, which the visitor may well consider small in relation to the area to be defended.

In the second siege Kemeys had 120 men but this time the Roundhead artillery was more powerful and achieved early successes. The steady bombardment eventually breached the wall near Marten's Tower, and the garrison, whose morale was appallingly low at this time, began to make their escape through it. Kemeys died in the final assault. After the Restoration in 1660 Henry Marten, one of the signatories to Charles I's death warrant, was imprisoned in the neighbouring tower for twenty years, but apparently in comfort. The tower became known thereafter as Marten's Tower.

Pembroke still held out. On the other side of the country Colchester was also holding firm and from the north a Scottish army was moving down towards London. If Cromwell broke off the siege to intercept the Scots, the holders of Pembroke would emerge and south Wales be lost again. But if he did not, the Scots might reach London and matters would be worse still. Desperately he redoubled his efforts to make Pembroke surrender. His scaling ladders were too short and the walls so stout that the Roundhead artillery made little impression. The countryside was hostile to the Roundheads and at intervals the garrison of Pembroke made sudden vicious sorties which badly affected the morale of the besiegers. But if Roundhead morale was poor the physical condition of the garrison which had been beleaguered and shelled since 22 May was as bad. By 1 July the garrison was almost at the end of its resources of food and water, for the castle had not been adequately provisioned and the Roundheads had managed to destroy its precious sources of water. Now they were on biscuits and rainwater. There was no hope, but they held on. From the walls they could now see Cromwell's big guns being hauled into position. There was scarcely enough powder left to be able to direct fire at their gun crews. But day succeeded day and they did not surrender. Not until 11 July when the big guns were already knocking down the walls did the small but valiant garrison finally give up.

After the siege Pembroke was 'slighted', that is damaged so that it should not be used again; but even greater damage was caused by later neglect and plundering for building materials. Fortunately in 1880 Pembroke castle came into the hands of the first of three devoted owners, all of whom gave much money, time and thought to its restoration and presentation. The last of these conveyed it to the Pembroke Borough Council in 1959. The visitor will feel assured that the future of the castle is now in safe and responsible hands.

Two other remarkable sieges occurred at Denbigh and Raglan. Denbigh held off the Roundhead forces for thirteen months before surrendering in 1646 to Mytton. Raglan was besieged by Sir Thomas Fairfax and 3500 men in 1646. It was gallantly defended by the eighty-four-year-old Marquess of Worcester. At the beginning of the war he had been a very rich man but he contributed a million pounds to the Royalist cause and also paid for the defence of his own castle, at a cost of about £40,000. He was a resourceful amateur scientist and had invented a water cannon but there is no proof that he used it in this siege. Eventually on 19 August 1646 the castle surrendered, not because of the heavy bombardment and the frequent attacks, but because the whole garrison was at the point of starvation. The Marquess survived and lived to 86!

In addition to these sieges, each a battle in itself, there were battles in the open field. Fortunately we have documents and letters describing many of them. Some of the letters are signed but some writers preferred to remain anonymous. One, describing conditions in Shrewsbury when Royalist soldiers were billeted there in 1642, ends with 'Yours, whose hand you know.' He says, 'They ride armed, up and down, with swords and pistols, muskets and dragoons, to the great terror of the people, that we scarce know in safety to go out of doors. They take men's horses, break and pillage men's houses, both night and day, in an unheard of manner.' Hereford fared no better, and the local trained bands were called out to expel the intruders who claimed to be Royalists but seemed little better than common robbers. Around Radnor Prince Rupert was more popular. He received many gifts at Radnor Castle:

Some brought him pieces of plate of great antiquity, as might appear by the fashion thereof. The common people brought in provisions for the maintenance of his court such as young kids, sheep, calves, fish and fowl of all sorts and some sent in fat oxen. Everyone was striving for the credit and glory of his country to exceed in several expressions of generous liberality.

Meanwhile, the Marquis of Hertford had contrived to seize Cardiff Castle and also to recruit an army of seven thousand Welshmen. With this force he went first to Hereford, and next to Tewkesbury, which he planned to capture. Un-fortunately for his recruits he was as lacking in military experience as they were. He was opposed by a Roundhead force raised by the Earl of Stamford. An account of the battle appeared in a pro-Roundhead pamphlet published in November 1642.

The Marquis, the Lord Herbert, with the wild Welshmen, assuring themselves of an absolute victory and so, furiously with the horse, which were some of the Marquis's old cavaliers, they charged in front of the Earl's forces, who, nothing amazed with their violent encounter, allayed the heat of their courage by heating them with good store of lead about their hearts, out of their carbines, pistols and muskets. Yet the force of those demi-devils was so courageous that nothing could withstand their fury, but that they fell pell-mell into the body of our foot so that some men were slain on our side though more on theirs. My Lord of Stamford's own regiment, at push of pike, keeping off the horses, while his musketeers, through their buffs and corselets sent death into their bosoms.

Hertford's Welsh infantry lacked nothing in the way of dash and courage but more was needed here than the crude weapons they possessed. They had no artillery and their muskets were much older and less serviceable than those used by their opponents. The outcome was inevitable. One section of Hertford's army which had been exposed to steady musketry fire, broke and fled. The full weight of the Roundhead attack now fell on the cavalry and the Welsh foot. These gallantly fought on until one of their principal leaders, Lord Paulet, was shot. The cavalry now fled from the field leaving the hapless Welsh foot in the path of the advancing Roundhead cavalry. 1200 surrendered and were granted a free pardon but by the time this happened 2500 were already dead. It had been a very bloody battle and showed clearly that if there were going to be more encounters like it the cost in lives of this war would be enormous.

Another spirited engagement took place the following January at Nantwich when Brereton for Parliament, and Aston for the Royalists, both tried to capture the town. Brereton was said to have 150 men and Aston 400, but in practice the numbers were probably even. The encounter took place at 6 p.m., after dusk, on rough ground. Both sides discharged their artillery but achieved little. A cavalry charge caused more confusion but no great damage. Now all were packed so closely together in the dark that it was difficult to tell friend from foe; before the wearing of distinctive uniforms it was easy to attack a man of one's own side in mistake for the enemy, even in daylight. The battle here surged back and forth, with both sides using swords and battleaxes. Gradually the Roundheads obtained the advantage.

Sir Thomas, seeing how things went, fled (as we hear) on foot three miles and then got a horse on which he fled to Whitchurch. Sir Vincent Corbet crawled away on all fours, lest he should be discerned and then ran on foot bare-headed to Over, six miles. Many were dispersed in the field and divers found there the next day.

The following February the Royalists had their revenge. A Roundhead chronicler managed to describe the battle in a manner which foreshadowed those accounts of 'strategic withdrawals' which became familiar in the present century. He wrote:

'We retreated to the Heath to find better ground, considering we might suffer much but could make no execution upon them. Where we rallied new ground was not to be found there. Part of the army making a retreat, the rest followed. Not out of fear for the enemy durst not meet us on even terms, but to get home before we were nighted. The enemy by their scouts discovered about 700 of our club-men coming near them from the forest in good posture and suspected that we had wheeled to the left, while the others were ready to charge on the other hand which struck them with so much fear they fled to Chester.'

The Royalist version was slightly different. They reported 'The rebels held out not above one hour. There were killed between three score and four score, one whole company taken, who cried for quarter and gave up their matches (muskets); but three of the King's party being wounded and not one slain.'

Undoubtedly it was a Royalist victory but the discrepancy between the two accounts shows how difficult it is to arrive at an objective view of a battle.

As the war progressed battles became larger and fiercer. On 17 October 1643 a force of Royalists, mainly Welsh, under Lord Capel, met a Roundhead force under Sir William Brereton and Sir Thomas Myddleton at Prees Heath, near Chester. One account runs 'And then most of the horse and foot we had at Nantwich went out to face them and set upon them, and drove them into the churchyard and into Acton Church, killed four of them and shot more, and got some of their horses. And when they had got the churchyard, they shot very briefly and our men could do no good with them.' Earlier in the war neither side would have considered fighting in the churchyard, let alone the church; now both sides could justify any form of desecration or sacrilege on the basis that it was for the benefit of the 'true' religion.

All wars generate a succession of somewhat unlikely stories and the Civil War was no exception. In all probability the wilder fantasies were readily believed. After their reverse at Pembroke a number of Royalists took refuge at Haverfordwest 'and informed the commandant of the loss of the fort'. At which news it is reported Sir Henry Vaughan with the rest of the commanders began to rage and swear like mad men and as a bear robbed of her whelps, ran up and down the streets crying, 'Beat up our drums, gather our horse and foot together, for we will out this night and be revenged on the Round-headed Parliament dogs.' And having with this bravado drawn their forces into a body, being about 450, Sir John Stepney, the governor of that town, like a prudent overseer, went into the churchyard to see if he could discern our force's approach towards Haverfordwest. About half a mile from the town he discovered a herd of young black bullocks coming towards him. These homed beasts so amazed the Knight that, being afraid of his own shadow, his worship ran to the head of their forces and swore 'God's Wounds, the Roundhead Dogs are coming'; at which report they marched out of the town and calling to mind the valiant example of Lieut-General Carbery they wheeled about and ran away. The boys of the town, perceiving them running, fell on their rear and took from them sixty muskets.

The story, like many propaganda stories, soon acquired its own documentation. The herd of bullocks soon found an owner, a grazier called Wheeler. Why they – or Sir John Stepney – should have been on the road at night is left to the reader's speculation.

On 5 August 1644 Colonel Mytton and Sir Thomas Myddleton launched a surprise attack on Prince Rupert's own regiment, which was quartered at Welshpool. They captured 346 horses, fifteen officers and forty soldiers. 'Sir Thomas Dallison fled away without his breeches in which was found a letter which he intended to send to Prince Rupert the next day.'

The battle of St Fagans which took place on 8 May 1648 was probably the most important battle of the war. Major-General Laugharne, the Royalist commander, was a man of great skill and experience. The Royalists knew this only too well for before he had changed sides he had inflicted many defeats on those with whom he was now serving. Although the Royalist cause was not lost until Pembroke castle fell, victory at St Fagans would have prevented Pembroke being besieged at all. With widespread disaffection against Parliament, and the likely arrival of Scottish Royalists in the near future, the future of the Roundheads was beginning to look bleak. They still had plenty of men in the field but were now experiencing sullen or active resistance. Colonel Horton was trying to eliminate the last traces of Royalist resistance from central and west Wales, but he found himself confronted with the 'scorched earth' policy which the Welsh had so often inflicted on their enemies in the past. When he heard that a newly-formed Royalist army, consisting mainly of Laugharne's former soldiers, was marching east to Glamorgan, he hastened from Brecon to the nearest point at which he might intercept them. This was St Fagans, commanding the Ely river. He took up position on 4 May. Patrols soon established the fact that a large force was approaching. It numbered eight thousand but as it was weak in cavalry and not, for the most part, very well armed, it was not as formidable as it appeared. Laugharne had only just arrived to take command, and did not want an immediate engagement. In fact he withdrew a few miles and considered his tactical plan. The outcome was that he positioned his forces across what is now the St Bride's – Fairwater road, parallel with and just behind the Nant Dowlais stream. Horton, con-fronting him, was lined up just west of Pentrebane farm, and Oke/s dragoons were placed on each wing. St Fagan's castle, already obsolete, did not come into the battle at all. Unfortunately the railway embankment has changed the course of the Nant Dowlais stream.

The battle began at 8 a.m. with Laugharne sending 500 men across the brook. They were charged by fifty of Horton's cavalry and pushed back. It was poor country for cavalry as there were high hedges which no longer exist but Colonel Okey's dragoons, who were mounted infantry carrying pistols, managed to edge forward using their 'dragons' (or small pistols) to advantage. The pressure on the right gradually began to bend back Laugharne's line. The rest of the Roundheads now put in a tremendous thrust all along the front, gradually pushing back the Royalists. As the Royalists gave ground, Bethel's cavalry on the Roundhead right saw an excellent chance to make an encircling charge. The realization that they were about to be encircled caused dismay and a hasty retreat among the Royalists. Dismay soon turned to panic and the battle was lost. As with many battles there was more killing after the main engagement than in it. As the Roundheads caught up with the fugitives many swift desperate fights took place in which both sides fell. On the battlefield itself three thousand men threw down their arms and were taken prisoner. It had been a very good day for Horton's outnumbered, weary troops.

Chapter 10

THE BATTLE OF FISHGUARD

The battle of Fishguard which took place on 22 February 1797 has often been described as 'a battle which was not a battle'. Unfortunately, the fact that the circumstances were extraordinary does not make the conduct of the defenders any less creditable. In the first phase of the Napoleonic War, which was destined to drag on intermittently for another eighteen years, the French had made a bold bid to obtain command of the sea. It had failed, but they felt that much embarrassment and difficulty could be caused to England if they assisted in stirring up trouble in Ireland. Accordingly a force of 1400, carried in three frigates, set off to land in Ireland; however the plan was changed and instead it was decided to land in Wales. The force was commanded by an Irish-American named Colonel Tate, a man with a very unpleasant reputation. The invasion party were 'expendables' who were mainly released from jails for the purpose of the raid. They wore British uniforms, called themselves 'The Black Legion' and imagined that all Wales would rise to join them in a victorious liberation march which would include considerable plunder and rape on the way to London. They landed at Carreg Wasted Point on the north coast of Pembrokeshire and made their headquarters at Trehoweli Farm. The frigates then put out to sea and left them to carve their path to victory. The commander of the local yeomanry, the Fishguard Fencibles, was Thomas Knox and he refused at first to take the news of the landing seriously. He went to what he imagined was the scene, but, observing nothing, ordered the Fencibles to take no action. However, local people, annoyed at the pillaging by the Black Legion – which had already begun – attacked them. Foremost was a woman named Jemima Nicholas. Using a pitchfork she took several prisoners.

Lord Cawdor, the colonel of the Castle Martin Yeomanry, now joined in. He gathered together a force which included some of Knox's Fencibles. On 24 February this army of 600 deployed above Goodwick Sands. Militant Welsh women, wearing red cloaks and tall hats, gathered to watch. A few shots were fired and Cawdor ordered Tate to surrender. Tate at first refused, then laid down arms. The Welsh women who were carrying pitchforks and other weapons had to be restrained from executing the Black Legion summarily. Jemima Nicholas received no decoration for the gallant part she had played but the Pembrokeshire Yeomanry received the unique distinction of a battle honour on home soil; they were allowed to wear the word 'Fishguard' on their badge.

But the effects of the invasion did not end there. The news caused panic on the London money market and the government had to suspend payments in gold and silver. Instead paper notes were issued and declared legal tender. Subsequently, the printing of more and more paper money has proved a temptation few governments have been able to resist. As Colonel Tate and the Black Legion started it all off we may feel that perhaps Jemima and her militant Welsh women should have been allowed to punish them appropriately. Or perhaps they should have taken their pitchforks to London and had a word with the Chancellor of the Exchequer. Then they could have worn the words 'Downing Street' on their hats.

Postscript

A book about military history in Wales would not be complete without a reference to the great Welsh regiments, although their battle honours were won far away from the area covered by this book.

No nation has more cause to be proud of its regiments than Wales has of the Welsh Guards, the Royal Welch Fusiliers, and the Royal Regiment of Wales which was formed in 1969 by the amalgamation of the Welch Regiment and the South Wales Borderers.

Appendix 1

Welsh losses at Edgehill were keenly felt and produced the following poem, published in 1642,

In Kinton Green*
Poor Taffy was seen,
O Taffy, O Taffy;
Taffy her stood
To her knees in blood,
O do not laugh, ye;
But her was led on
With false Commission,
To her unknown;
That poor Taffy herself
Might live in health,
But her got blows for her wealth;
O Taffy, poor Taffy

Their grievous fight,
Did make day night,
O Taffy, Taffy;
Her would be flying,
Liked not dying,
'Twas bad Epitaphe;
Her sword and spear
Did smell for fear,
And her heart were
In a cold plight;
Made Taffy outright,
His poore britches besh – te,
O Taffy, O Taffy.

The guns did so f—t,
Made poor Taffy start,
O Taffy, O Taffy;
Her go bare foot,
Then so go trot,
O do not laugh, ye;
For her was bang'd,
Because her had gang'd,
Under the Command Of Array.
Who had for her pay
Many a sound great knock that day,
O Taffy, O Taffy.

Her go in frieze,
Eat bread and cheese,
O Taffy, O Taffy;
Feed with goats,
Without old groats,
O do not laugh, ye;
Had you been there,
Where her did appear,

With cold cheer In Knapsack,
You would then alack,
For fear have turn'd back,
O Taffy, O Taffy.

Her will now invent
How to repent,
O Taffy, O Taffy;
And for want
Of words to recant,
O do not laugh, ye;
For her will be swore,
Her will do no more,
Though her be poor;
And too true
Valour her will shew,
No more in such great crew,
O Taffy, poor Taffy.

Her do conclude In doleful mood,
O Taffy, O Taffy;
Her will weep To goats and sheep,
O do not laugh, ye;
For her be anger,
And then hang her,
If in danger;
Her come,
Pox upon a gun,
Has spoiled her going home,
O Taffy, poor Taffy.

Kineton is the name of the village at the base of Edgehill

(From a pamphlet entitled 'The Welshman's Public Recantation, or her hearty sorrow for taking up arms against her Parliament, etc.' Printed at London for Fr. Coule, 1642).

Appendix 2

DOCUMENT OF 1644

An Attempt to Besiege Chirk Castle by Sir Thomas Myddleton, its owner, Christmas 1644.

MAY IT PLEASE YOUR HIGHNESS,

This gentleman, journeying towards Oxford, I most humbly beseech leave to present to your Highness by him an account of a late action of the rebels. They lately besieged me for three days; their engineers attempted to work into the castle with iron crows and pickers, under great planks and tables which they had erected against the castle-side for their shelter, but my stones beat them off. They acknowledged in Oswestry they had 31 slain by the castle, and 43 others hurt; their prime engineer was slain by the castle-side; they are very sad for him. If your Highness please, this gentleman will fully impart all the passages during the siege to your Highness; he was in the castle with me. I shall not presume to be further tedious. I most humbly kiss your Highness's sweet hands, and will ever be

Your Highness's most humble
And assuredly faithful servant,
JOHN WATTS

Chirk Castle, December 25,1644.

To his Highness Prince Rupert, humbly present this.

The original is at Chirk Casde, in the possession of Mrs Myddleton-Biddulph. Mercurius Aulicus, referring to this event, states that it was Sir Thomas's intention to keep Christmas in one of his own houses:

He came therefore before Chirk four days before Christmas, with his two brothers, Cols. Mytton and Powell. He would not abuse the castle with ordnance (because it was his own house), but fell on with fire-locks at a sink-hole where the Governor, Col. Watts, was ready to receive him; and gave a pretty number admittance (having an inner work within that hole), but when he saw his opportunity, he knocked them all down that came in, and with muskets killed of the rebels 67, wounded many more, and beat off Sir Thomas, who became so enraged that he plundered his own tenants.

Appendix 3

DOCUMENT OF 1645

Further particulars of the Attempt to Regain Cardigan Castle by the Royalists under Gerard. January 22.

The most considerable exploit that hath been performed in any of our armies since my last was by Lieut.-Col. Powell and Col. Laugharne, near Cardigan Castle, in Wales, against Gen. Gerard, the particulars whereof on Thursday, Feb. 6, was thus advertised.

The enemy having intelligence that there was a great want of provisions in the castle, whereof Lieut.-Col. Powell was Governor, Col. Gerard having gathered all the forces he could to besiege it, for that purpose marched towards it with a great party, and in his march intercepted some boats of provisions that were going to their relief. Upon his approach and sitting down before the castle, having by a stratagem got possession of the town, he sent in by a trumpet a menacing summons to the Governor, requiring him in his Majesty's name to surrender the castle, with all ordnance, arms, and ammunition therein, unto him, together with the provisions [prisoners] therein, for the prisoners who were taken therein of Col. Gerard's, whereof I gave you an account some weeks since, remained there; and further threatened the Governor that if he would not surrender it by a day which he named, he would not give quarter to him or any of his soldiers, with some other haughty and lofty expressions to that purpose. Upon the reading of this summons, the gallant Lieut-Colonel called his officers and soldiers together, and used many notable encouragements unto them to behave themselves like brave spirits, further telling them that whereas Col. Gerard threatened to give no quarter, he would neither give nor take quarter, adding that he would rather feed upon those hides (there being 300 in the room which he pointed to) before he would starve, and that those who loved him would do the like before they would yield to the enemy, and thereupon, by the concurrence of his officers and soldiers, he sent the enemy an absolute denial, and in the meantime got an opportunity to send to Col. Gough [must be Laugharne] to come with a party to his relief. Upon this the enemy broke down the bridge between Cardigan and Pembrokeshire, that so no relief might come, and fell to making their batteries and planting their ordnance against it [the castle], for the storming of it, which they endeavoured to do oftentimes, but were still repulsed, losing about 150 men upon their several onsets. While the enemy were in this posture, Col. Laugharne came out of Pembrokeshire to the relief of the castle, but when he came to the bridge, he found it was broken down, which was some impediment unto him; whereupon he caused an arrow with a letter to be shot into the castle, to give them notice he was coming, and that they might sally out upon the enemy the same time he fell on. After this, leaving the horse behind them, the foot soldiers (being led by this their valiant Commander, who told them that if but an hundred went he would lead them on) making use of faggots and other pieces of wood, got over the river and fell upon the rear of the enemy, and those in the castle falling upon them at the same time, the enemy were quickly put to the rout; 200 of them slain on the place, four brass pieces of ordnance, 600 arms, and 150 prisoners taken. The chief of the prisoners were Major William Slaughter, Capt. Nicholas Butler, Capt. Richard Pryse, Dr. Jeremy Taylor, Lieut. Thomas Barrow, Lieut. Morgan Mathewes, Ensign Edward Barrow, and others.

I have been more particular in this success, in regard the malignants did the beginning of this week report with much confidence that Col. Gerard had totally routed Col. Laugharne's forces, taken Cardigan Castle, and reduced several places in Wales: cujus contrarium verum est.

Appendix 4

The Siege of Raglan conducted by Lord-General Fairfax

Sir,

In my last I acquainted you with the General's leaving of Bath and coming in person to the siege before Raglan, where he was entertained with great acclamation by the soldiers. After which he sent a summons to the castle, to which a dilatory answer, though not an absolute denial, was sent. A civil reply was made to it, and after a day's consideration the Marquis took occasion to write a calm letter to the General, expressing how much he did respect the General's family, and what long acquaintance he had with his grandfather; in conclusion, invited to have some propositions sent him, which were accordingly sent. The conditions were honourable for the soldiery, but as to the Marquis himself [he was] to submit to the mercy of Parliament. The Marquis having considered of these, remained doubtful whether the Parliament would confirm what the General should grant, in case they should agree, to which the General returned answer, assuring him that what he concluded of, would be performed. Whereupon, Thursday, August 13, the Marquis sent out a drum, desiring leave to send out his Commissioners on Friday, at 10 o'clock, whereupon, he said his Excellency should see he would not be an obstruction to peace, which we conjectured was as much as to say, he would send a positive answer to our propositions. And thereupon the drum was returned, with a safe-conduct for the Commissioners' coming forth, and a cessation of arms from ten o'clock till three. The Commissioners appointed on our part to meet theirs were Col. Birch, Mr. Herbert, one of the Commissioners of Parliament residing with the army, and Major Juliday [or Tuliday] whose commission was to receive what they should deliver, and present it to the General.

I shall now give you an account how near our approaches are made unto the castle. That which is our main work is about sixty yards from theirs, and that is the most. We have planted four mortar-pieces, each of them carrying grenade shells, twelve inches diameter, and two mortar-pieces, planted at another place, carrying shells about the like compass; so that in case the treaty do break off we are then ready to show by what extremity they must expect to be reduced. This we are very confident, that the grenadoes will make them quit their works and out-houses, and solely betake themselves into the castle, which will be a work of time before we are able to undermine it, in regard we must mine down the hill under a moat, and then their works, before we can come to the castle. Yet we conceive it feasible to be done with some loss. Our engineer, Capt. Hooper, a painful and honest man, with exact running trenches, which are made so secure as if they were works against a storm, will (with God's blessing) come within ten yards in a few days, and then I believe we shall make galleries, mines, and many batteries. The General is every day in the trenches, and yesterday appointed a new approach, which the engineer of this army, returned from Worcester, is to carry on with all expedition.

During the parley yesterday, which held from nine till two, they permitted us to come to their works, stand close to their stockades and trenches, and discourse with them; so little do they regard our knowledge of their works. The propositions sent out by the Marquis yesterday were as high as ever any garrison yet propounded, to which the General sent a short and positive answer, letting his Lordship know his propositions deserved no answer, and as for himself he must expect no other conditions but to submit to the mercy of the Parliament, and gave him time till this day at 10 o'clock to receive his final answer. We are all persuaded if he could but have leave to go beyond the seas, the soldiers having honourable conditions, he would submit; and were it not better to grant a man of 84 years these terms, that probably will be in his grave before the affairs of Parliament will give leave to call him to trial, and thereby save the fives of many an officer and soldier who have adventured their lives in the Parliament's cause, than to gain this old man's carcase at so dear a rate? Col. Rainsborough is already come to the Leaguer, and Col. Hammond is this day expected. The Marquis hath this morning sent word that he will treat upon the General's propositions. Whereupon, the treaty is appointed at Mr. Oates's house, about a mile and a half from Raglan, where it is to begin this afternoon at two o'clock. The General's Commissioners are Col. Morgan, Col. Birch, Mr. Herbert, Quarter-Master-General Grosvenor, Lieut.-Col. Ashfield, and Major Juliday. By the next you shall hear further from

Your assured friend and servant,
W.C.

Usk, August 15th, 1646.

The Surrender

Sir,

On Wednesday last, Aug. 19 [Raglan] Castle was surrendered to his Excellency, Sir Thomas Fairfax. The enemy were no sooner marched forth but his Excellency entered the castle, took a view of it, and had some conference with the Marquis, and afterwards went that night to Chepstow, where he was liberally entertained by the Committee, and came from thence yesterday to Bath.

The Castle of Raglan was as strong a piece (as I have seen) encompassed with a deep moat, besides the river. There were in it near 500 officers, gentlemen, and soldiers (a list of the chief of whom I have enclosed). Divers of the officers and soldiers refused passes, saying that they could go anywhere without passes, so that many of them are not comprised in the fist; twenty pieces of ordnance, not above three barrels of powder; but they had a Mill with which they could make a barrel a day, which would supply them sufficiently. There was in it also great store of com and malt in several rooms, the true quantity whereof I cannot give you. There was also a store of wine of all sorts, and beer. The horses they had left were inconsiderable, and those almost starved for want of hay, of which they had none, and not many oats, so that the horses ate their own halters for want of meat, and were tied with chains. Those who marched forth had not the least uncivility offered them by the soldiers, who (as formerly during this War) were very punctual in observing the Articles.

Your real friend and servant,
W.C.

Bath, August 21, 1646.

Articles for the Surrender of the Castle

1. That the castle and garrison in Raglan, with all ordnance, arms, etc., shall be delivered without wilful spoil unto his Excellency, Sir Thomas Fairfax, or such as he shall appoint to receive the same, on Wednesday next, the 19th day of this instant August, by 10 o'clock in the forenoon, in such form as shall be expressed in the ensuing Articles.

2. That upon the said 19th day of August, the officers, gentlemen, and soldiers of the garrison, with all other persons therein, shall march out of the said garrison with their horses and arms, with colours flying, drums beating, trumpet sounding, matches lighted at both ends, bullets in their mouths, and every soldier with twelve charges of powder, match and bullet proportionable, and bag and baggage, to any place within ten miles of the garrison where the Governor shall nominate; where, in respect his Majesty hath no garrison in England, nor army anywhere in the Dominion of Wales, their arms shall be delivered up to such as his Excellency shall appoint to receive them, where the soldiers shall be disbanded, and that all, both gentlemen and soldiers, shall have the benefit of these Articles, except persons excepted from pardon and composition – they engaging themselves not to bear arms against the Parliament, nor do anything during their abode in the Parliament's quarters prejudicial to their affairs.

3. That all such as desire to go to their homes or private friends shall have the General's pass and protection for their peaceable repair to, and abode at the several places they shall desire to go unto; the officers and gentlemen to pass with their horses and arms, and all with bag and baggage.

4. [Officers and gentlemen to have three months to make peace and compound with the Parliament – passes to be given to such as should desire to go beyond the seas, provided they go within three months of the surrender.]

5. [Sick and wounded to remain in the castle till recovery.]

6. [All officers, gentlemen, and soldiers, to be protected from being questioned, affronted, plundered, or injured, during the said three months; such as break any of the Articles above to be punished]; and that all these Articles may be faithfully observed, according to the true intent thereof, without any cavil or mental reservation to infringe them, or any of them.

Note the privileges: 'matches lighted at both ends, bullets in their mouths'.

Horton's Account of the Battle of St Fagans

Letter to Lenthall, Speaker of the House of Commons

Sir,

I shall give you a narration (according to my own observation, and the help of some of the officers with me), both of the manner and success of our late engagement with the enemy, near St Fagans. The enemy having drawn off from Saint Nicholas to Llancarvan, Penmark, and Fonmon Castle, Friday, the fifth of May. On the Lord's Day, at night, they advanced towards us again to St Nicholas; by which we did presently apprehend that they intended to fight with us, and were induced to such a belief, the rather, because they knew two days before that Lieut.-General Cromwell was coming towards us. This made us draw in all our horse close that night, as we had done divers nights before, and prepare for the work in the morning; and about seven in the morning our scouts discovered their body about a mile and a half from our quarters, upon which we drew out, and took the best ground we could. Major Bethel commanded the horse on the right wing, Major Barton on the left, and Colonel Okey and his Major with the Dragoons on both wings with the horse. The enemy advanced fast with a strong forlorn of foot and about six Pickering horse; Lieutenant Godfrey with a forlorn of 30 horse and 20 dragoons charged and routed them, doing good execution, which gave us the advantage of a new ground; so we advanced with horse and foot upon them, Capt. Garland with two hundred fire-locks on foot, and Captain Nicholets (this bearer), with Colonel Okey's own troop of dragoons, mounted with some horse on the right wing, disputed the first encounter very hotly, where he showed much resolution, and beat the enemy out of two closes and over a little brook, and there maintained their ground under command of the enemy's shot, until the forlorn of foot commanded by Captain Lieutenant Fann, and some horse from the left wing, came to their relief; and then they beat the enemy from hedge to hedge before them, until they came to a bridge where the enemy's greatest body were placed. The horse all this while and dragoons following this first success with much vigour, were constrained to stand the enemy's shot for some time before the foot (though they made great haste) could come up to them; and presently the first division of foot, commanded by Lieutenant-Colonel Read, fell close up to the enemy's front; Major Wade with the second division got over die little brook on the left flank of the enemy; Major Barton likewise, with the left wing of horse, with much celerity passed over a boggy place and the little brook to second those foot; and some of the enemy's horse coming on to charge the foot, were gallantly resisted and beaten back by Captain Hughes. By this time the horse and dragoons on the right wing were gotten over also, the enemy's foot standing very stoutly to it, until our horse began to surround them, and then they presently all ran, and we cleared the field, our horse and dragoons pursuing them for eight or ten miles. The enemy's horse, which they say were five hundred, were employed in their rear to keep up their foot, and we never saw after we were engaged, above sixty horse in a body all the fight. Their whole number of horse and foot is confirmed to be about 8000 – they had about 2500 musketeers by their own confession, besides bills, pikes, and clubs. We took up the day we fought above 2000 fire-arms, with pikes, Welsh bills, and other weapons great store, ten barrels of powder, and all the rest of their ammunition in the field, and most if not all their colours. The number of prisoners that are taken are about 3000. (I have here enclosed a list of officers as they gave in themselves to the Marshal.) Some hundreds of them were disarmed four or eight miles from the place we fought, which we let go. Captain Wogan, a Member of the House of Commons, sent down by them into these parts, carried himself from the first to the last with great resolution, encouraging the soldiers and engaging himself in the head of the service. Captain Jones, who came off from the enemy to me long since, with a troop of sixty horse, behaved himself likewise very well, as also all other officers and soldiers, who I can truly say kept their order in the performance of their service to the admiration of the enemy, as some of them confessed.

And that God's mercy may be the more magnified in this late happy success over our enemies, I think it now season-able to make known unto you the straits we were in, and difficulties which compassed us about; we having a potent enemy lying within two miles upon much advantage of ground, before us the high mountains, close to us on the right hand the sea, near unto us on the left Chepstow taken and Monmouthshire beginning to rise in our rear, besides our great want of provisions and long and hard duty, all which seemed to threaten our sudden ruin. That God should please in this condition so to own us, as to make a way for us through the midst of our enemies, and to scatter them every way is a mercy not to be forgotten, especially by those who have more immediately tasted of it. Witnessing the truth of these things as they are herein expressed by

Your faithful and most humble servant,

Tho. Horton Bridge-end, May 13, 1648.

Appendix 6

EXTRACT FROM ROLL OF ARCHERS FROM THE LORDSHIP OF BRECKNOCK WHO SERVED AT AGINCOURT

List supplied, by Lt-Col. F. Field, MBE, RRW

David ap Howell ap Gwillelm Lloyt Ieuan ap Eynon Bach
Ieuan ap Morgan ap David ap Me
John ap David Dew
Geffrey Baret
David Tormour

IN THE OFFICE OF THE BAILIFF ITENERANT
Howell ap David Lloyt ap Jake
Rys ap Phillip ap Llewelyn
Deykyn

Ieuan Dwy ap Howell ap Griffith Raulff
Ieuan Dwy Irroyr
Thomas ap John ap Jake Gam
David Maur ap Howell
Walter ap Llewelyn Goch
Llewelyn Vycha ap Llewelyn Yarlle
Howell ap Ieuan ap Rees
Howell Mawr
Griffith ap Ieuan Vaughan
David ap Griffith Goch
Meredith ap Llewelyn ap Ieuan au Llewelyn Ddwy
Llewelyn Ddwy ap David Lloyt
Howell ap Me ap Griffith Vachan

Ieuan ap Griffith Lloyt
Eynon ap Griffith De
Rosser ap Howell ap Griffith ap Madoc
Ieuan ap Griffith Bach
Ieuan Ddwy ap Rosser
Thomas ap Griffith Bloith
Watkyn ap Jake Lloyt
Griffith ap Ieuan ap Howell Veyn
John Wheler
David Dew ap Howell ap Griffith ap Madoc
Geffrey Dene
Ieuan ap Jenkyn ap Griffith ap Madoc
Ieuan ap Trahan ap Gwalter
Llewelyn ap Rustogyn
Ieuan Bach ap Glyn Goydour
Glyn Dew ap David Ddwy
Griffith ap Ieuan ap Howell ap Jenkyn
Willim Waldebeff Capellanus

IN THE OFFICE OF THE SHERRIFF
David ap Coch ap Ieuan Mathevey
Ieuan Melyn ap Ieuan
Rosser ap Ieuan ap Codogan
Griffith Fordyn
Jankyn ap Llewelyn
Phillip Lloyd
John ap Gurgen
Howell ap David ap Graham
Ieuan Tew ap Gwillim Routh
David ap Ieuan ap Coffe
Yanthlos
Ieuan ap Res Carpenter
Res Weythe
John Wynter
David ap Meredith Bywell
David Coke
Trahan ap Madoc
Morgan Dry Leche
Llewelyn ap Ieuan ap Morgan
Howell ap Ricard
Ieuan Ferour Cum Equi Cwm Watkin Lloyt
Meredith ap Trahan ap Ieuan Vachan
David ap Teuan ap Howell ap Eynon
Res ap Gwillim
Ieuan ap David Gwyn

YSTRADFELLTE
Morgan ap Madoc
David Coch
David ap Ieuan ap Llewelyn
Morgan ap Griffith

Griffith ap Gwalter ap Res
Res ap Me Lloyt
David ap Ieuan Vachan
Ieuan ap Howell ap Griffith ap Raulffe
Llewelyn ap Howell ap David ap Res
Trahan ap Res ap Cadogan

ORDNANCE SURVEY MAPS

All the maps are O.S. First Series. 1974.

Chapter 1. Battles of Pre-History
Sheet 114 (Anglesey)
Barclodiad is at 378 708, i£ miles from Rhosneigr. Per-mission to visit should be obtained from 22 The Square, Caernarvon.
Caer Twr is at 219 831. Open always.
Caer Leb is at 473 674 and is open always. Note the marshy surroundings making this a good defensive site.
Bryn Celli Ddu is at 508 702. Open weekdays and Sunday afternoons. Apply at the nearby farmhouse.
Castell Bryn Gwyn is at 465 671. Open always.
Sheet 123 (Lleyn Peninsula)
Tre'r Ceiri (the town of the giants) is at 373 446, near Llanaelhaem. Take the B4417 or the road from Llithfaen. Sheet 115 (Caernarvon and Bangor)
Dinas Dinlle is at 437 563, on the coast. Note the strength of the double ramparts.
Craig y Dinas is at 448 520.

Chapter 2. The Battles against the Romans
Sheet 171 (Cardiff and Newport)
Caerleon is at 340 907. There is a small but interesting museum close to the site. Visitors will probably want to follow this visit with one to the National Museum of Wales in Cardiff and to the Welsh Folk Museum at St Fagans (II5 714)-
Kenchester, originally Magnis, is on the Roman road at 436 428.
Sheet 137 (Ludlow and Wenlock Edge)
Caer Caradoc Hill is at 478 955, close to the A49, north-east of Church Stretton. There is no reason to suppose he built either this or the other Caer Caradoc at 310 758 but there is every reason, as well as persistent local tradition, to suppose that he used it.

Visitors to the battlefield of Clunbury Hill should start at Craven Arms and go along the B4368 in the direction of Clun. As they move along the Clun valley they will notice a number of traces of ancient fortifications, some of which are marked on the ordnance survey map. It is a fascinating area for the archaeologist and the military historian, for it must have been the scene of many unrecorded battles of which evidence may yet come to light. For Clunbury Hill turn left at Little Brampton and the road will take you across the Kemp and the Clun which join a mile east of Oaker. Note the fortifications of Oaker Wood.

Having crossed the stream (with less difficulty than the Romans) and passed through the village, you are almost immediately confronted with the steep hill up which the Romans forced their way protected with the testudo.

The battle site ranges from 371 813 to 375 801.

Sheet 126 (Shrewsbury)

Wroxeter (Viroconium) is at 565 085. Although all this area is now Shropshire it was Briton territory till the building of Offa's Dyke. Shrewsbury (Pengwem) was formerly the capital of Powys.

Sheet 117 (Chester)

To follow Ostorius Scapula's invasion route of the north begin at Mold at 240 643 and proceed to Denbigh and St Asaph on Sheet 116 (Denbigh and Colwyn Bay). Denbigh is at 050 660 and St Asaph at 035 745.

Chapter 3. The Battles for Supremacy

Sheet 146 (Lampeter and Llandovery)

The Dolaucothi gold mines are at 665 404. Pencader, the site of Griffith ap Llywelyn's victory is at 444 362.

Sheet 117 (Chester)

Very little variation was possible in the invasion routes of Wales owing to the nature of the terrain. The traditional invasion route was close to the A55 from Chester, passing Hawarden at 320 655 (note Hawarden Old Castle; Hawarden castle is a later residential building), Ewloe, where the castle at 290 655 is somewhat oddly sited (approach via the track over the field on the right hand side of the road), and Flint 247 736. Flint was important long before Edward built the castle which is still impressive here. Beyond Flint is Cefn Coleshill at 225 735 and this is the reputed site of Henry II's reverse against Owen Gwynedd (Chapter 5). Due south of Flint is Mold, strategically sited in the river valley at a road junction. Holywell is a little further on at 184 765 on Sheet 116.

For Offa's Dyke you need seven maps: 114, 117, 126, 137, 148, 161, and 162 but all will be useful for other battle areas too. The northern end of the dyke is at Gop Hill, an ancient burial mound on Sheet 116 at 086 802 although the dyke path will take you all the way into Prestatyn. Anyone planning to walk the dyke should obtain Offa's Dyke Path by C. J. Wright (Constable).

Chapter 4. The Battles against the Normans

Sheet 161 (Abergavenny and the Black Mountains)

Abergavenny is at 229 140 but the castle is a shadow of its former strength and is more impressive from the outside than from within. Castle Arnold was at 317 101 which is near Llansabbath and close to the A40. Skenfrith is on the B4521 at 458 203. Grosmont is at 405 245 (on the B4347) and covered a larger area than that indicated by the present remains. Whitecastle is at 380 167 and is best approached from the B4521 (the Skenfrith – Abergavenny road). It is not easy to find but it is well worth the trouble for it is the perfect example of a fighting man's castle.

Ewyas Harold is on Sheet 149 (Hereford and Leominster) at 385 287 which is close to the A465. All that remains is a high mound somewhat overgrown. Richard Snailham, the explorer, who has travelled the Zaire river, the Blue Nile, the Blue Mountains, etc., camped on it one night recently and found it an eerie and disturbing experience.

Other castles mentioned in the text may be found as follows:

Clifford on Sheet 148 (Presteigne and Hay-on-Wye) at 243 457. Private, but permission to visit may be obtained.

Wigmore on Sheet 137 at 408 693, behind the church, much overgrown but remarkably formidable even in ruin. Just off the A4110.

Deganwy is on Sheet 115 (Caernarvon and Bangor) at 783 794. Turn off the A546 at York Road.

Rhuddlan is on Sheet 116 at 024 780. Once greatly neglected and ruinous, it is now beautifully maintained.

Cilgerran is on Sheet 145 (Cardigan) at 196 431. Of obvious military strength but also extremely picturesque and much beloved of painters.

Coity is on Sheet 170 (The Rhondda) at 923 816, close to Bridgend.

Kidwelly is on Sheet 159 (Swansea and the Gower) at 409 070.

Ogmore is on Sheet 170 at 882 769.

Carew is on Sheet 158 at 046 038.

Pembroke is on Sheet 158 at 980 016.

Manorbier is on Sheet 158 at 064 978.

Chapter 5. The Battles of Owen Gwynedd

Griffith ap Rees's victory over the Normans in 1136 probably took place in the middle of Cardigan on land which has now been built over but there is a tradition that it took place at Banc y Warren on Sheet 145 at 205 475. Undoubtedly a battle took place here but it may not have been Rees's. A tumulus was built on the top of Crugmore and soon attracted many legends; one was that armour left there overnight would be found broken in the morning and another that the tumulus frequently changed shape.

There had been a battle at St Dogmael's five years earlier at 142 456, when Llywelyn ap Iorweth had fought David ap Owen to decide who should rule Cardigan. David lost 4000 infantry and 500 cavalry- all of whom were said to have been mounted on grey or silver horses. Llywelyn lost 650 infantry and 250 cavalry. All are said to be buried under the rocks.

The campaigns of Owen Gwynedd against Henry II in the north ranged over sites already mentioned and identified. Sometimes the site of a battle, otherwise unrecorded, may be identified by a name such as Gwydyr or Gwaed-dir, which means 'the place of blood'.

Oswestry is on Sheet 126 at 295 310. Battles here probably took place around the Iron Age fort known as 'Old Oswestry5. Chirk Castle is also on Sheet 126 at 268 381; it is perfectly preserved, is lived in by the Myddleton family who have owned it for nearly four centuries, and welcomes visitors. Nearby Crogen Windys is where Henry II was defeated by a combination of endless rain and Welsh courage which made 'a crogen5, the name for a desperate victory against the odds.

The remains of Basingwerk Abbey are at Greenfield on Sheet 116 at 195 775.

The remains of Margam Abbey are on Sheet 170 at 801 862.

Dolwyddelan Castle (Llywelyn's birthplace) is on Sheet 115 at 722 523.

Chapter 6. The Battles of Llywelyn ap Iorweth (Llywelyn Fawr)

Most of the places where Llywelyn ap Iorweth fought have been referred to in previous chapters. In addition: Rhayader is on Sheet 147 (Elan Valley and Builth) at 969 680 but no trace now remains of the castle, which is thought to have been close to the church.

Llanstephan Castle is on Sheet 159 at 351 101. There is no convenient car park here.

Narberth is on Sheet 158 at no 145.

Haverfordwest is on Sheet 158 at 953 157 and now encloses a museum and art gallery.

Chapter 7. The Battles of Llywelyn the Last.

Dinas Bran is on Sheet 117 at 224 431. It overlooks Llangollen and the A539.

Criccieth is on Sheet 123 at 499 376.

Builth is on Sheet 147 at 045 510. Visitors to the battle site of Orewin Bridge will no longer find this name nor even the bridge. The site is the now demolished Hendre bridge which may be reached by taking the A483 from Builth. At Cilmeri just beyond the Prince Llywelyn Inn you will see a monument on the left of the road. This records the spot where Llywelyn is thought to have been killed. The battle was a little further on. One mile beyond the monument there is a path leading under the railway bridge on the left hand side. This descends to the river where there are old stone supports and the stumps of wooden posts. The bank is steep but levels off just where it begins to ascend the ridge. Hendre means a winter homestead and clearly has no connection with the battle. Were it not for the local tradition the Gwarofog bridge at Garth, two miles further along this road, would fit the facts we know of this battle rather than Hendre does and is worth an inspection; the bridge itself is, of course, a recent one. Cilmeri is at 005 515 and Hendre at 995 509.

Dyserth is on Sheet 116 at 061 799 and is on private land.

Dynevor is on Sheet 159 at 615 225.

Drysllwyn is on Sheet 159 at 554 205.

Carreg Cennen is on Sheet 159 at 668 191.

Newcastle Emlyn is on Sheet 145 at 315 406.

Moel y Don, where Edward was repulsed, is on Sheet 115 at 519 679 (half way along the Menai Strait).

Harlech is on Sheet 124 (Dolgellau) at 578 313.

Caerphilly is on Sheet 171 at 168 868.

Conwy is on Sheet 115 at 785 775. The battle of 1295 probably took place at 773 778.

Caernarvon is on Sheet 115 at 475 626.

Chapter 8. The Battles of Owain Glyndwr

The Pilleth battle site is on Sheet 148 (Presteigne and Hay-on-Wye) at 255 684 on the eastern slope of Bryn Glas, not in the valley as shown on the Ordnance Survey map. Take the 4356 from Presteigne. The burial pit was under the clump of trees in the middle of the field, and the whole battlefield may be seen clearly from the road. It was said that some of the archers in the English army changed sides and turned their arrows on to their own men, but as the whole area must have been very overgrown in 1402 it does not seem that this can have had much effect in a battle which was mainly a surprise ambush.

Ruthin is on Sheet 116 at 122 578. The castle is now a hotel where medieval banquets are served regularly. Dolbardan Castle where Glyndwr imprisoned Lord Grey of Ruthin is on Sheet 115 at 586 598 (close to the A4086).

Machynlleth, where Glyndwr held his Parliament, is on Sheet 135 at 745 009. Also on Sheet 135 is Aberystwyth at 578 816. There is also a fort at 585 805 and an early castle at 589 781.

Monmouth is on Sheet 162 at 510 130 and still has a very fine example of a fortified bridge.

Chapter 9. The Battles of the Civil War

Ellesmere is on Sheet 126 at 403 346 but the castle is now a bowling green. There is also a bowling green on one of the baileys at Clun. Welshpool is on Sheet 126 at 232 073.

Raglan is on Sheet 161 at 415 085 and Chepstow is on Sheet 162 (Gloucester and the Forest of Dean) at 534 941.

St Fagan's battlefield is on Sheet 171, at 783 779. Take the A4119 from Cardiff and turn off towards Fair- water. The entire battlefield may be observed from the Fairwater- St Bride's road, which runs through it.

Chapter 10. The Battle of Fishguard

Sheet 157 (St David's and Haverfordwest). Carreg Wasted Point is at 931 405 and Goodwick Sands will be found at 945 380.

Appendix 8.

The Map Gallery

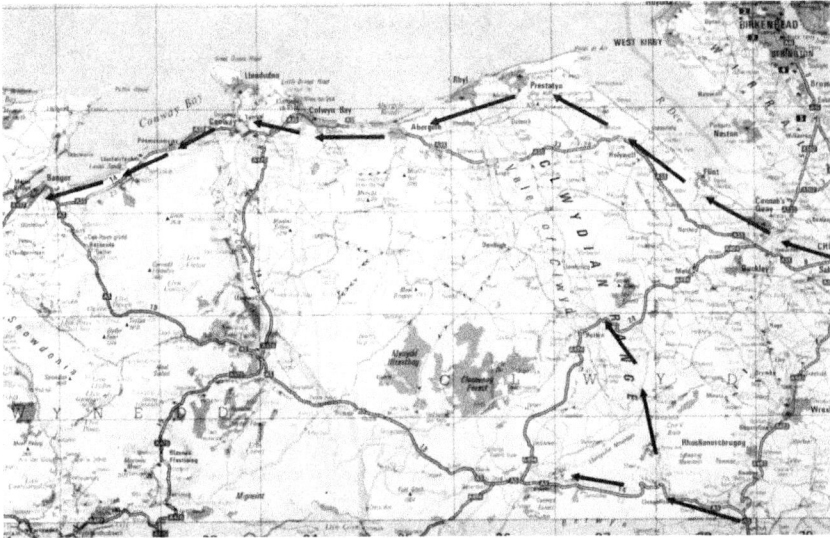

Map I – North Wales – possible invasion routes

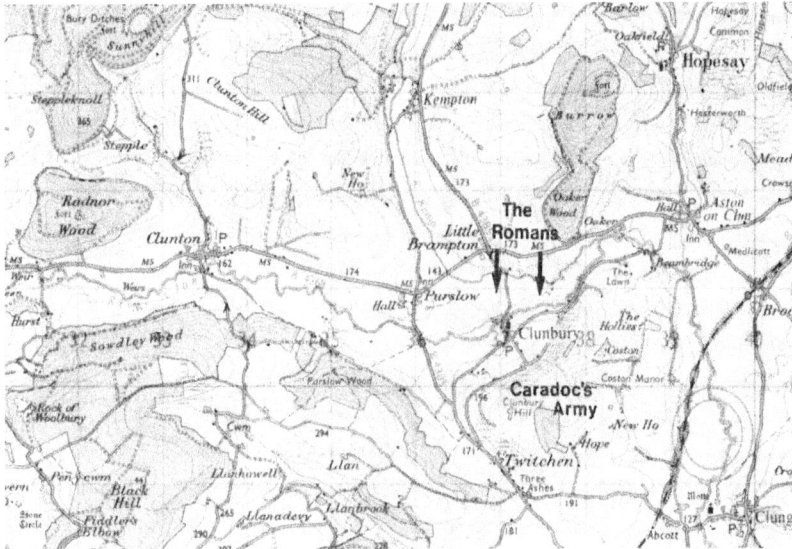

Map II – Clunbury Hill, AD 51

Map III – The strategic position of Caerleon

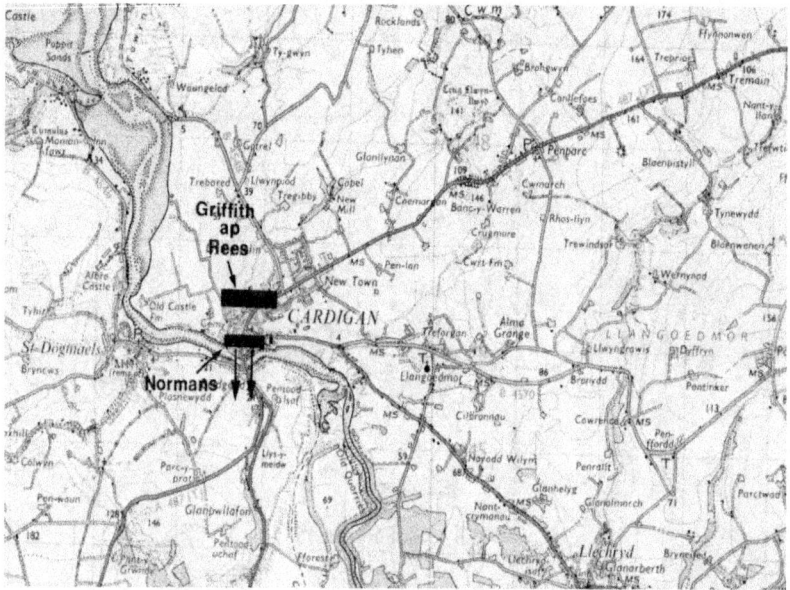

Map IV – Cardigan, 1136

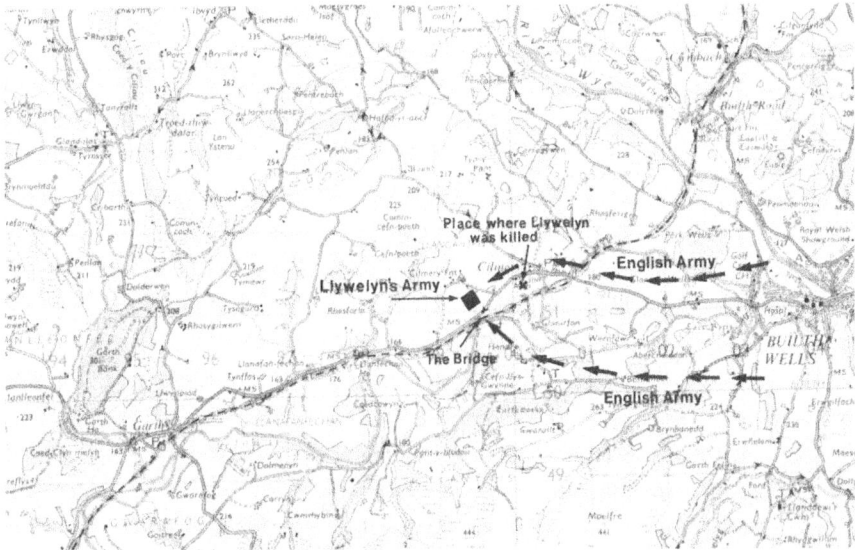

Map V – Orewin Bridge, 1282

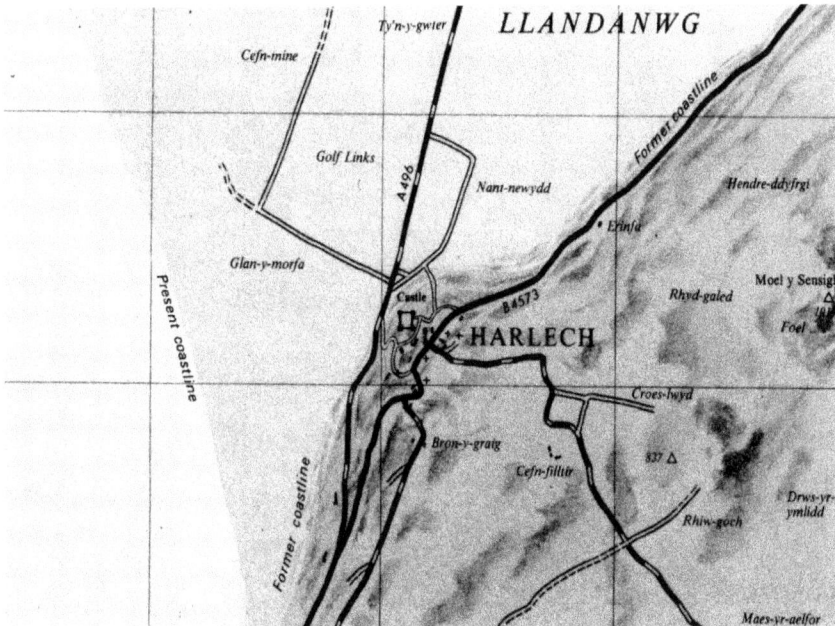

Map VI - Harlech Castle – then and now

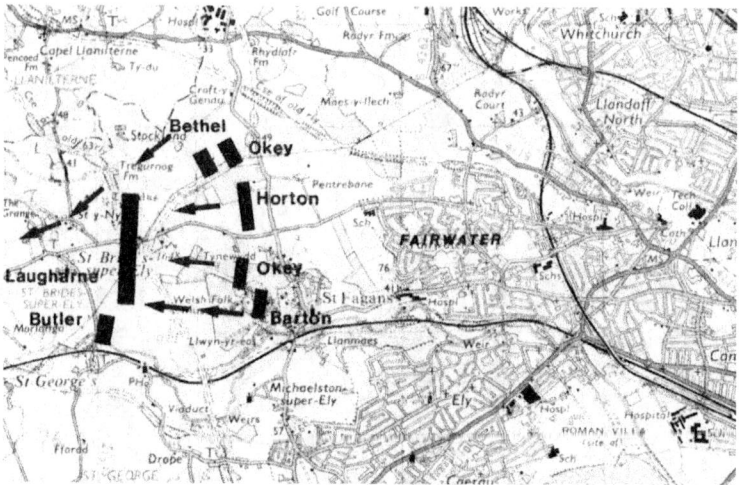

Map VII – St Fagans, 1648

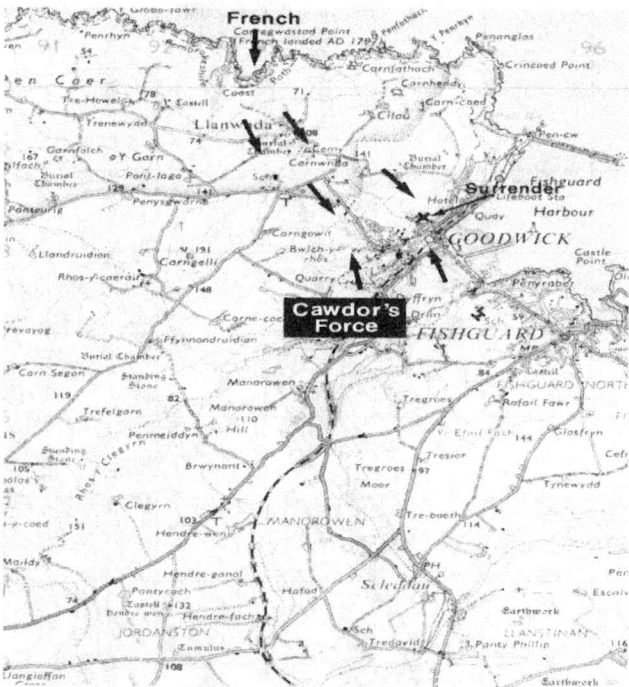

Map VIII – Fishguard, 1797

'Historians are like deaf people who go on answering questions that no one has asked them.'
Leo Tolstoy

The true worth of an individual is valued in many ways but for an historian how can we know their worth? I think many would agree that it is an ability to ask and answer questions that many would shy away from. Tolstoy would certainly agree with that and one of the finest military historians England has produced in the 20th Century Philip Warner ably matches this description.

His style is engaging but absolutely honest. He will not sugar coat when the bitter facts need to be faced. He will make an allowance for the stresses and needs of war but he will explain them for what they are not for what the victor would rather they be.

Below is not a formal biography but a personal tribute given by his son, Richard Warner, at his funeral. It's a marvellous piece of explanation and devotion that illuminates the man and his work:

I rang the Book Review Editor of *The Spectator* last week to tell him that Philip had died and therefore please not to send more books to review. I introduced myself as 'Richard Warner, Philip Warner's son'. He replied 'that is a very nice thing to be able to say'.

He was absolutely right and it does feel very nice, doesn't it, to be a child of Philip's, or a member of Philip's family, or one of Philip's much cherished friends and work colleagues, and indeed nice to have enjoyed Philip's stimulating company.

He prized above all the loyalty of family and those firm friends who he included inside that inner circle. Once you had won his trust and respect, then you were on his side and he would do anything for you. 'Families stick together through thick and thin'. You didn't let the side down. If one did, he would be slow to forgive and never to forget.

So, as his family and friends, I welcome you all here today to the Royal Memorial Chapel, to join in this Service of Thanksgiving for Philip.

Philip did not 'meekly hand in his dinner pail', as P. G. Wodehouse put it – he remained an active, alert, interested and interesting man right to the end.

He died just under a fortnight ago, aged 86, on September 23rd, peacefully in his sleep, beside his great love and companion for the last 30 years, Freda. He had gone to bed with a copy of *The Spectator*, in which he had written a review of a biography of a hero of his – Jock Lewes, co-founder of the Special Air Service. He had finished his day as he always did, reading a chapter from Wodehouse. He just did not wake up to make the early morning tea.

He was – in his words – 'going like a train' (an expression he had learned before the era of Connex South Central), enjoying a very busy life in his fourteenth year as the army obituarist on *The Daily Telegraph* (he had filed his last obit on the day before), a regular book reviewer for *The Spectator, The Field*, and many other papers and periodicals.

It is perhaps only in the last fortnight that the Warner family has come to realise what a special man our father was, and just how many facets there were to his life. Each of us has found out more about this reserved, steadfast, lively-minded and inspiring man from letters or telephone calls since his death.

He had special, private, individual friendships with a large number of you – but since he did not talk about himself, the facts of his life are not well known. When teaching us to box, he encouraged to 'present a moving target' – and he took this advice better than anyone. When his close friends and next door neighbours of some forty years found out only from his obituary in the *Telegraph* that he had been a Prisoner of War, let alone a guest of the Japanese, I realised we need to – in his words – 'establish some facts'.

Philip was born the youngest child of three and the only boy into a farming family in Warwickshire, deep in the countryside, on May 19th 1914, just four months before the First World War.

Philip proudly traced his ancestry back some 500 years in the same county, loving this continuity with the past that he picked out in his first book, published in 1968, *Sieges of The Middle Ages*:

'Standing on the battlements of a castle the humblest person feels a sense of power and grandeur. He is back in the past and feels a kinship with the original owners. In all probability this kinship is genuine, though remote. Every family that was in England in 1087 is now related thirteen times over to every other family in the country at that time; he is thus related both to the mighty baron and the most downtrodden villein.'

The Warner family sold their farm in 1924, which meant that Philip had to put up with poor local schooling, making him determined that his children would have the opportunity of public school education that he had missed – never mind whether he could afford it or not.

He strongly believed that 'nothing is impossible, you can do anything, if you put your mind to it – and persevere at it'. His achievement in winning a County Major Scholarship from Nuneaton Grammar School, against all expectations, to Christ Church, Oxford, was a prime example.

Another example lay in his sporting achievement: undaunted by his isolated upbringing on a remote farm, and realising that his elder sisters were not interested in Rugby Football, he acquired a Rugby ball and a coaching book from the library: by practising assiduously in fields, he made himself into an excellent place kicker. Likewise he developed into a ferocious tackler, with a tackle bag made from old sacks and hung from a tree. This tackle bag did double duty as a punch bag, while he taught himself to box.

By the age of eighteen, he had played as a Wing Forward for the Leicester first team. He then went on to play for a great range of teams – Blackheath Moseley, Saracens, Windsor and principally for the Harlequins, in addition to two-timing two County sides, Sussex and Berkshire 'it seemed much easier to play for them both than to explain the mix-up' he unconvincingly claimed with that mischievous twinkle in his eye.

Despite irrefutable evidence to the contrary, Philip did not think of himself as an excellent Rugger player, or boxer (he boxed for the Army) or athlete (he represented his County and the Milocarians), or squash player (for the Jesters' Club). He never mentioned his own contributions – he thought only of the team's achievements and the spirit in which the game was played.

After spending an idyllic year of University sporting and social life as an undergraduate of Christ Church in 1933, he received a nasty jolt, when the authorities sent him down for omitting to pass his exams. 'Always learn from experience' he said, and did, taking care never to make the same mistake again. Rapidly finding himself a job as a prep school master, he won a scholarship to Cambridge in 1936 and graduated from St Catharine's College in 1939.

The impending war soon broke and Philip enlisted in the Royal Corps of Signals. [It gave him great pride forty years later to write the regimental history *The Vital Link*, at the request of General David Horsfield and with his collaborator Colonel Robin Painter.]

He saw action in the Far East, defending Malaya and Singapore island, where he and 60,000 other Allied troops were compelled to surrender to the Japanese and became a Prisoner of War for three and a half years.

That he felt betrayed and frustrated by the Allied command and the treachery and complicity of the politicians can be seen in his 1988 book, *World War II: The Untold Story*: 'for the British Government, and for Churchill in particular, it was an incredible disaster; to those who had been trying to make a fight of it the whole campaign had been a major exercise in frustration. The final insult was that the world blithely accepted the Japanese figures for the numbers who had surrendered and the absurdly inflated figure of 130,000 passed into history – in fact the true figure was 60,000'.

You would not find Philip making this statement anywhere else, as he would not talk about the past. He did however write about it revealingly – as in *The Fields of War* (1977) – 'When fighting soldiers eventually read or hear what was supposed to have taken place on campaigns in which they were engaged they tend to smile cynically. Sometimes they consider offering a few corrections, but rarely bother; the task, they often feel, is too large, and scarcely worth the trouble.'

As a PoW, Philip drew his strength from his background and his upbringing. He kept himself as fit and healthy as he could, remained resolutely positive in outlook and inspired his comrades with his unflagging belief that they would pull through.

To raise morale he organised theatrical productions and skits. Without props, scenery, paper, with people at the end of their powers of endurance, he still managed to put on entertainments to cheer the troops, to the complete incomprehension of the Japanese guards.

In one talk, a man who had been employed as a butler in a grand household described his day, eating meals both before and after waiting on the family 'he had two breakfasts, elevenses, two luncheons, high tea twice, and of course two dinners before absentmindly munching the dog biscuits he had pocketed as he took Her Ladyship's Chihuahua out for its nightly walk'. This to a rapt audience of PoWs whose daily ration was half a cupful of rice.

At the end of the war, Philip weighed four and a half stone, but he had survived. He set about building a new life, first at The Treasury, then at the British Council in Spain.

In 1948, with a young wife Patricia, and a newly-minted daughter, Diana (my brother and I were still ideas) he became a Junior Lecturer at the newly established RMA Sandhurst. This occupation of lecturing to young and stimulating young cadets – as well as the ideas that they gave back to him – fitted his abilities perfectly. He firmly believed and communicated that 'you could learn anything, if you put your mind to it' and that 'everybody was best at something, it was just a question of finding out what it was'. His forward leaning walk and his leadership by example appealed to cadets. He worked here for 3I years until his retirement, relishing his colleagues, the intake of cadets, the opportunities for sport and for coaching, and the grounds.

And to a man who was committed to the principle of working and playing 'full tilt', he relished the chance that the Sandhurst academic terms gave him to use 'what would otherwise have been my leisure' for his other interests.

Thirty one years amounts to more than a third of his life. During this time, he rose to be senior lecturer, teaching many intakes of cadets about politics and current affairs.

He immersed himself in the Academy's sport: he ran the Rugby XV and taught goalkicking to the then current England full back, John Willcox. He ran the athletics too, watching with immense satisfaction when his protégé, the Ghanaian Kotei, qualified for the Olympic high jump at the Sandhurst Athletic Ground, still wearing his track suit top.

He loved the relaxed concentration that fly fishing on the Sandhurst lake demanded. Deeming it a suitable activity for cadets, he would declare regretfully to each new intake that – as he was both the Secretary of the Fishing Club and the person responsible for deciding who passed their exams – the lists inevitably got muddled up. This rapidly boosted membership.

It would be a matter of great delight to him to know that Sandhurst has given permission for his ashes to be scattered over the pool on the Wish Stream named after him (the 'Plum' pool), where he fished only a month ago. 'How marvellous' he said then, 'to be able to still tie on a fly and to cast a good distance – and I'm 86!'

He relished teaching generations of cadets about both current affairs and how to communicate – till his time a neglected subject. He enjoyed drawing out from each individual what made him tick, habitually asking each new student to talk for a brief time in front of the class on subjects of their choosing. Cadets responded such diverse subjects as how to soft boil an egg and how to remove the top from a bottle of champagne in one blow from a sword.

Whatever the subject, the aim was to give self-confidence to these young officers. Eventually, it led to his founding a new and now thriving department of Communications. Begun as a small section within the Department of Political and Social Studies in 1973, it now has transformed into one of the three Academic Departments within Sandhurst's training.

Philip's great break came in 1967, at a time when he very much needed one: overburdened with school fees and with a very ill wife (Pat was to die in 1971), he took with both hands an introduction to a book publisher provided by his friend and Sandhurst colleague, Brigadier Peter Young. He never forgot this kindness and determined to repay Peter's faith in him. Seizing his opportunity of a contract and an advance, he saw a way to pay for his children's education and proceeded to write two books a year 'from a standing start' for the next twenty-five years.

That was a fantastic achievement – 150,000 published words, aside from the pages he crossed out or rejected, plus all the historical research – 3,000 words a week, every week for quarter of a century. 'You have to keep pushing the pen across the paper' he would say.

Every one of those words was lovingly and meticulously typed, and retyped if he wished, by Freda. It was just as well, as only Freda could read Philip's handwriting, which resembled most of the time the tracks of inebriated and exhausted sand eels, improving for a brief period every few months as he laboriously worked from a *Teach Yourself Handwriting* manual.

Many of the fifty or so books he has written have – to his great delight – come back into print in new formats as military classics. He felt that they were good books, his earnings from Public Lending Right reflecting library borrowings showed how often they were taken out, and now even publishers have seen the light. 'Never underestimate the stupidity of publishers, Dickie.'

Though each book was a massive labour – he would just say 'toil and swink', each one allowed Philip to describe events through the eyes of the soldier at the time, rather than looking 'with the benefit of hindsight'. In the *Crimean War* (1972), he says: 'Equally full of martial spirit, strategic foresight and tactical ability are critics who have never heard a shot fired in war, never endured hunger, thirst, heat or cold, and never commanded anyone, in war or peace, in their entire lives'.

This constant theme informed his biographies of unfashionable subjects, whose leadership styles he admired: for example, General Brian Horrocks 'The General who led from the front' and Field Marshal Claude Auchinleck 'The Lonely Soldier'.... lonely he may have been, but he had the vision which allowed the SAS to get started.

This empathy with his subjects and his ability to pick out the essential character of the people he wrote about led to a life and career that can be looked back on not only with great affection but an historian's eye for truth – no matter where the awkward facts might lead.

Philip Warner – a concise bibliography

Philip wrote many books across the military range. The following titles are being re-published as both print books and e-books. Please contact us with any queries:

Alamein
Auchinleck – The Lonely Soldier
Battle of France 1940
Battle of Loos
Best of British Pluck
British Battlefields – A complete Compendium
British Battlefields – Vol 1 – The South
British Battlefields – Vol 2 – The North
British Battlefields – Vol 3 – The Midlands
British Battlefields – Vol 4 – Scotland & The Border
British Battlefields – Vol 5 – Wales
Battlefields of The English Civil War
Battlefields of The Wars Of The Roses
Crimean War
Dervish: The Rise and Fall of An African Empire
Distant Battle
D Day Landings
Famous Welsh Battles
Field Marshal Earl Haig – The Enigma
Fields of War – Letters Home from The Crimea
Firepower
Growing Up in the First World War
Guide to Castles in Britain
Guide to Castles in Britain (Illustrated)
Harlequins
Horrocks – The General Who Led From the Front
Invasion Road
Kitchener – The Man Behind the Legend
Medieval Castle
Passchendaele
Phantom
Secret Forces of World War II
Sieges of the Middle Ages
The Soldier: His Life in Peace and War
Special Air Service, The SAS
Special Boat Squadron, The SBS

Stories of Famous Regiments, The
World War I: A Chronological Narrative
World War II: The Untold Story
Zeebrugge Raid

All the material in this work is protected by copyright © 2014 Class Warfare.

All rights are reserved. No part of this publication may be reproduced or transmitted in any form or by any means including but not limited to electronic or mechanical including photocopying, scanning, recording, internet or any information storage and retrieval systems without direct permission from the publisher.

The right of Philip Warner to be identified as the author was asserted by him in accordance with the Copyright, Designs and Patents Act 1988.

www.ingramcontent.com/pod-product-compliance
Lightning Source LLC
LaVergne TN
LVHW021542080426
835509LV00019B/2789